The Basset Hound Owner's Survival Guide

The Basset Hound Owner's Survival Guide

Diane Morgan

HOWELL
BOOK
HOUSE

New York

Howell Book House
A Simon & Schuster Macmillan Company
1633 Broadway
New York, NY 10019

Macmillan Publishing books may be purchases for business or sales promotional use. for information please write: Special Markets Department, Macmillan Publishing USA, 1633 Broadway, New York, NY 10019.

Macmillan is a registered trademark of MACMILLAN, Inc.

Library of Congress Cataloging-in-Publication Data
Morgan, Diane. 1947–
    The basset hound owner's survival guide / Diane Morgan.
    p. cm.
    ISBN 0-87605-018-6
    1. Basset hound.   I. Title.
SF429.B2M67   1998
636.753'6—dc21 97-28743
    CIP
Manufactured in the United States of America
10 9 8 7 6 5 4 3 2 1

CONTENTS

PREFACE

Hippolyta: *I was with Hercules and Cadmus once*
When in a wood of Crete they bayed the bear
With hounds of Sparta. Never did I hear
Such gallant chiding; for, besides the groves,
The skies, the fountains, every region near
Seemed all one mutual cry. I never heard
So musical a discord, such sweet thunder.

Theseus: *My hounds are bred out of the Spartan kind*
So flewed, so sanded, and their heads are hung
With ears that sweep away the morning dew;
Crook-kneed and dewlapped like Thessalian bulls;
Slow in pursuit, but matched in mouth like bells,
Each under each. A cry more tuneable
Was never holloed to nor cheered with horn
In Crete, nor in Thessaly. Judge when you hear.

Midsummer Night's Dream (act 4, scene 1)

Obviously William Shakespeare knew his Bassets. (In case you're wondering, "flewed" refers to the dewlaps, and "sanded" to the color.) In this glorious paeon to our breed, the Bard makes reference to all the most salient aspects of the Basset: The sweeping ears, the crooked legs, the slow, deliberate pursuit of game, and the musical "sweet thunder" of his cry.

This book, too, in its own humble way, is a paeon to our breed. It will focus on some of the characteristics even Shakespeare seems to have missed: The exquisite beauty and nobility of the Basset, the tender solemnity of the soulful eyes, the exquisitely sculptured head, the noble expression, and the thick globs of drool gleaming on the kitchen floor.

Note: For convenience sake, I have used the male pronoun throughout when referring to the Basset. Take no offense if your dog is a bitch.

ACKNOWLEDGMENTS

Basset Hounds are not for the many—but for the mad. I thought I was all alone in my wild and shameful passion for this breed until, one fateful day, slogging through the mire of the Internet, I found Basset-L, a newsgroup for disturbed people like myself caught in the unholy grip of Basset-mania. I signed on and found salvation.

Basset-L became, for me at least, a combination of multiple pen pals, an advice column, a laugh a day, and group therapy. It is to the contributors of Basset-L, and to their noble refusal to get professional help, that this book is dedicated. I'd like to thank Nancy Gallagher, administrator of the online newsletter, *The Daily Drool,* as well as the members of that group, for providing additional stories and insights. I'd also like to thank Amanda Pisani, my kind and patient editor at Howell Book House, for her valiant efforts on this project.

Thus: To all the members of Basset-L, *The Daily Drool,* and their beloved pets, both present and departed. To Duster, Rosie, and Chelsea; Gus, Fern, and Molly; Credence, and Max; Spencer, Flash, and Watson; Mr. Mumbles, Katsie, and Darwin; Freckles, Mr. Willie, and Sasha. To Pepper, Whiskers, and Buffy. To Herne, Droopy, and Wilhelmina. To my own Bassets—Mugwump, Miles, and Ruby. To Rhoda, Dapper Dan, and Becky. To Duchess, the grande dame of *The Daily Drool.* And to Katy, who was so horribly abused and neglected because she was not a "favorite dog," and to Gretchen Laffert who rescued her and tried so hard to save her life. Maybe most of all, to our late and beloved Miss Xanadu, centerpiece of Basset-L, who recently had to leave us for the Rainbow Bridge. Officially, Miss Xanadu was Gretchen's dog, but in truth, she has been in the heart of all of us. We miss you, Xanny.

Thanks to all of you.

INTRODUCTION—
Or Why Get One of Those
Things in the First Place?

O scar Wilde once said, "All art is useless." Pretty much the same thing has been said about Basset Hounds. Like fine art, Basset Hounds are for connoisseurs, and basseteers are the true connoisseurs of dog ownerdom. Bassets are not conventional pooches. To the uninitiated, Bassets are neither classically beautiful, utilitarian, or "doglike," but we know that the Basset Hound is a discriminatingly intelligent, supremely huggable, noble, courageous, and ultra-civilized dog. He is a true individualist, with a super-excellent disposition and a devoted, honorable nature. He bears discomfort with the stoicism of Marcus Aurelius—well, actually, as I was writing this, Ruby stole Miles's squeaker toy and set him to crying.

But otherwise, they are very brave animals indeed. Bassets are wonderful with children, friendly but reserved with guests, and willing to either lie around all day like rugs or take to the woods with you at a moment's notice. What more could one ask?

However, it must be confessed right away: **The Basset has a dark side.** Behind the floppy ears and soulful eyes lies the Beast Within.

Bassets smell. They roam. They drool. They're a LOT bigger than they look. They are notoriously hard to housebreak. They're stubborn. They eat and sleep at marathon levels. They're practically useless as guard dogs. (Mine barely wake up when the family comes banging through the door, exhausted after a day's work, hoping for the cold wet comfort of a friendly nose. As a matter of fact, the dogs look faintly annoyed that their beauty rest is being disturbed.) On the other hand, the Basset's hearing is preternaturally acute when it comes to the sound of a candy bar being unwrapped—no matter how quietly.

Who wants a dog like this? If you admire the beauty of the Irish Setter, the sophistication of the Poodle, the loyalty of the German Shepherd, the exuberance of the English Springer Spaniel, or the cleverness of the Border Collie, well, go ahead and get one of those dogs. There's no accounting for taste.

But, if you have a sense of humor, like a challenge, and really know how to live life, then a Basset is for you!

ONE

The History of the Beast

The noble Basset Hound waddles right into the Dark Ages

Basset beginnings are shrouded in the mists of history. Of course, this is true of most things, but Bassets are so low they are downright cloaked in invisibility. Bassets are said to be originally descended (and descended they have—in lineage, stature, and character) from St. Hubert's Hound. Some modern authorities, having examined ancient sources such as Arrian and Oppian, place a variety of Basset Hounds even earlier than St. Hubert, way back to the second century. Oppian and Arrian, however, were not so clear as they might have been, and it's difficult to determine exactly what breed of dogs these early writers were describing. So we'll just stick with St. Hubert. He's always been good enough for me.

Perhaps you have been wondering all this time about St. Hubert. Even if you haven't, I'm going to tell you about him anyway.

St. Hubert was the so-called apostle of the Ardenne. His date of birth is unknown, but he died in 727. His feast day is November 3, which is the day after All Souls' Day, which follows All Saints' Day, which of course follows Halloween. It's therefore no accident that Halloween is a favorite holiday for basseteers, who like nothing better than to dress up their dogs on this day and frighten the neighborhood.

St. Hubert story as told by shadow puppets

Halloween is a favorite day for basseteers. Here is Gracie, Pam Posey-Tanzey's Basset Hound, among lesser beings.

We know little about Hubert's childhood, but as a young man he spent his time dashing around in the forest of Ardenne, consorting with the pagans, who were still worshipping oak trees and having a generally good time in the woods. During this period, before he became a saint, or indeed even a Christian, Hubert spent many idle hours hunting and trapping helpless little animals, and it was this rather unsavory hobby that led, curiously enough, to his conversion.

While hunting one fine Sunday afternoon (some sources say Good Friday), he came across a stag in the forest, in whose antlers gleamed the cross of Christ. This would be bound to have an effect on anyone, and it converted Hubert on the spot. (Actually, the same story is told about St. Eustace, but since it has now been pretty well agreed that St. Eustace was a fictitious character, Hubert gets the stag horns all to himself.) According to the story, Hubert flung himself to earth and asked for guidance. The stag, probably hoping to get rid of Hubert for good, told him to leave the forest to seek instruction from Lambert, the local bishop. Hubert did as he was told, and the rest is history, or at least hagiography. The stag, therefore, is the emblem of St. Hubert.

Under Bishop Lambert (who was eventually canonized himself), Hubert had a good start on the road to sainthood, despite his later connection with Basset Hounds. Lambert, you may recall, was murdered in 705, probably at the instigation of Pepin of Herstal, a truly awful man who had had it in for Lambert ever since the good bishop rebuked Pepin for having an affair with his own sister-in-law. None of this, however, concerns Hubert, so we'll just skip the juicy details.

St. Hubert died as a result of a boating accident of some sort, the exact details of which are cloudy at best. It's always tempting to blame the demise of Hubert on the Basset, but there really doesn't seem to be a connection.

Even though he became a cleric, Hubert never completely rid himself of the hunting bug. Consequently, the monastery of which he was abbot took to breeding hounds, and it was this group who developed the St. Hubert's Hound, named of course for their beloved abbot. (Because of this connection with dogs, by the way, Hubert's name is sometimes invoked as a charm against rabies. It doesn't work very well, however. It's better to get the shots.)

This is how the Basset enters history. (Perhaps you thought I would never get to this part.) In eighth-century France, the forests, as you may imagine, were deep and wild, not to mention tangled. The original St. Hubert's Hound looked much like the present-day Bloodhound, and while it possessed an unequaled nose, it was simply too big to go groping about in the underbrush. Enter the Basset, whose appearance on the scene had been preceded by many years of careful breeding, as well as a little luck, by the good monks of St. Hubert's. The Basset is essentially a genetic mutant, afflicted with dwarfism. He is short enough to get under any bush, which is just what the monks wanted. Both the St. Hubert's Hound and the Basset Hound were bred to trail, but not to kill, their game. The monks wanted to do that themselves. Soon enough, the joys of basseteering caught on, and the breed left the monastery behind to join the nobility. (Actually, all this stuff about St. Hubert may be wrong. Martha Knight writes that a prehistoric Basset may have been the ancestor of *Tyrannosaurus rex*: note the big head, at least one pair of short legs, the voracious appetite, the

Bassets were bred to trail, but not to kill, their game. (Miles, Dick Weber)

constant scavenging, and the never-ending drool. The split in the family tree probably occurred when *Tyrannosaurus rex* got nasty while the Bassets continued to be sweet tempered.)

In those fabled days, the well-hounded gentleman was possessed of (or by) no fewer than 12 of these noble beasts. (Although being possessed by Basset Hounds is no worse than being possessed by the devil, neither is it any better.) At any rate, it was apparently the height of style for the aristocratic owner to follow along after his hounds in a little cart, nicely furnished with bottles of claret and ham sandwiches.

Bassets may have been used originally to hunt European badgers, an easier mark than our own feisty American species. An American badger would demolish a Basset. Why the badger should be such a prized item, as its fur is not particularly valuable and its flesh is inedible, is a mystery.

The Basset Hound first acquired international fame in 1863, when it was a major hit at the Paris Dog Show. Of course, lots of other things were happening that year; the American Civil War was in full swing and saw the battles of Chancellorsville and Gettysburg. That was also the year that Archduke Maximilian of Austria was proclaimed Emperor of Mexico.

These trivial incidents pale, however, before the Great Basset Coup at the Paris Dog Show, when the Basset swept all before him.

There were at least two types of Bassets common at the time, basically divided into rough (Basset Griffon) and smooth coated (Basset Francais). They were further divided into very short, crook-legged hounds (Basset à Jambes Tordues), hounds with longer, straighter legs (Basset à Jambes Droites), and a compromise version (Basset à Jambes demi-Tordues). One has to be French to remember these names, let alone pronounce them, but it is good to reflect on the Basset's complex and oh-so-continental background.

The Basset Hound (in the guise of the Basset d'Artois) was first introduced into England in 1875 by Sir Everett Millais; the Kennel Club recognized the Basset as a separate breed eight years later. The dog was an immediate success at the Wolverhampton Dog Show, and the English Basset Hound Club was founded in 1884.

Later on, Queen Alexandra, wife of Edward VII, took a great fancy to the breed and showed them successfully herself. Of course, knowing what Edward VII was like, anything would have been an improvement. Edward has been seriously accused by some of having been Jack the Ripper. He was not Jack the Ripper, but since he had to spend most of his adult life as Prince of Wales opening bridges (his mother, Queen Victoria, refused to allow him to see state papers or go on visits to foreign dignitaries), no one would have blamed him much if he had been.

Long before King Edward's day, though, Basset Hounds came to America. It is said that General Marquis de Lafayette brought them to this country as a gift to George Washington. (It is not recorded what General Washington thought of them—or indeed what he did with them.) It may be Washington who first referred to the Basset as the "old Virginia bench legged beagle." Then again, it may not. Bassets have many faults, but they are NOT Beagles.

As a side note, Washington's fellow Virginian, Thomas Jefferson, apparently scorned the lowly Basset Hound. Instead, he kept Briards to look after his sheep. This worked out all right most of the time, but every once in a while, the Briards would eat the sheep instead of guarding them. This irritated Jefferson, and he used to complain about it in his journal.

The American Kennel Club recognized Bassets as a breed in 1885. The first American-registered Basset was a tricolor named Bouncer, a very nice sort of name, I think. There ought to be more Bassets named Bouncer in his honor.

The current American breed standard was accepted in early 1964, with revisions made later to emphasize the utility of the breed. All present-day American and English Bassets are descended from a pack of 15 pairs sold to Sir Everett in 1882 by Lord Onslow. (This is the place to discuss Lord Onslow's other contributions to history, but they are too well known, as well as too numerous, to mention.)

Sadly, the Basset's glory days at the Paris Dog Show have never been equaled in modern times, and the Basset Hound has not, so far, been awarded a Best in Show at Westminster. This, however, is merely an example of the shortsightedness of the judges. It's also probably for the best, since honors of this kind almost inevitably lead to a soaring popularity, something that is not in the best interests of any breed. It's far better to keep the secret joys of Basset owning to ourselves.

Basset Acquisition

There was a young man from Wiscasset
Who had one incredible asset.
It hung low; it was long,
Now don't get me wrong,
I am speaking, of course, of his Basset.

How does one acquire a Basset Hound?

Basset Hound owners come in two basic types. First, there are those like myself, who have always dreamed of owning Basset Hounds. When I was kid, I always went to sleep Christmas Eve thinking that this Christmas for sure, I'd find a cuddly Basset puppy under the tree. My dream, however, did not come true until I became an adult, mostly because everyone I lived with until then belonged to the "Why do you want one of those things?" category of human beings—in other words, the unenlightened.

These folks are the second category of Basset Hound owners. They have had Bassets thrust upon them, almost always having been worn down in the end by people of the first category. Curiously enough, owners from this second group generally turn out to be the most caring and fanatical Basset owners of all, once they get used to the idea of owning a Basset in the first place.

Some of us have always wanted a Basset for Christmas. Rosebud and Daisy, owned by Beth Fuller, are dressed for the occasion.

The problem for type number one people is how to convince type number two people (usually, but not invariably, husbands) to become Basset Hound Owners (B.H.O.s). Good advice comes from Anita Wright:

> Get in touch with your local rescue group. When they tell you they have one that will suit you, you have to mention it **all the time**. Relate all the cute things you have been told. Soon he will feel that the Basset should be home with you. The clincher: **Tell him it is going to be his dog.** Terry was quite excited about Mumbles, even before he arrived. Now all I hear is "My dog this, my dog that." And talk about preferential treatment. Mumbles is a real cutie, and a real "buddy boy." He follows Terry everywhere, slobbers all over him, and all I hear is how **his** dog is a real little boy dog and how wonderful he is. Of course Watson [the senior dog] knows where he stands in the order of things, so he just lets it all go by. They really are good friends now, too.

Unfortunately, dear Mr. Mumbles has since passed away. He is heartily missed by all of us.

From Jennifer Jamieson:

I found out about a rescue that needed a home (after Rob had said, "NO more pets.") However, he went with me to see the dog—"just to look," I said. Of course he fell in love with him as he saw him trying to jump through the glasstop table to get to an open box of pizza. I guess he realized this was his "soul (dog) mate," and we brought him home the next day. Rob seemed to like the thought of having his own dog, especially since now there would be two boys (er . . . I mean men) in the family now. One just drools a little more than the other.

Jennifer does not explain which one is the drooler. (Basset drool is discussed in more detail in the home decorating section of this book.)

Most breed experts and people who work in humane endeavors agree that the selling of dogs by pet stores is an unsavory activity that should be, at the very least, discouraged. Many pet store dogs have been poorly bred, malnourished, and taken from their mothers at an unconscionably early age.

Jennifer Jamieson's husband is glad to have a buddy in her Basset, Shorty.

What is a puppy mill?

How do you recognize a puppy mill when you see one? There are several telltale giveaways. First of all, puppy mills **always** have puppies for sale, something that is just not the case with reputable breeders. Reputable breeders breed "occasionally," when they believe they can produce an excellent litter. Beware of people who have permanent signs attached to their property proclaiming, "AKC puppies for sale." The AKC does **not** register or certify breeders or kennels; simply because a puppy is registered or registerable with the AKC is no guarantee of the puppy's quality, or the conditions under which he was bred and whelped. Equally, the words "champion bloodlines" mean nothing. Most AKC dogs have champion bloodlines, if you go back far enough. If you want champion bloodlines, make sure that your prospective dog's parents are champions. Further back than that means nothing.

Puppy mills frequently deal with several or even many breeds. Reputable breeders seldom deal with more than one or two. It's simply not possible to keep up with more.

Puppy mills frequently maintain filthy conditions. The kennels may be dirty, and the dogs may be unkempt. Always demand to see at least the mother of the litter, and take careful note of her condition, especially her coat and claws. The latter should show signs of clipping, and the coat should be clean.

Puppy mills are not involved with actively showing dogs. The owners will be unknowledgeable about Bassets and unfamiliar with their specific needs. Be informed yourself. The more you know, the less easily you'll be fooled.

Puppy mills ask no questions of prospective owners. Conscientious breeders will ask you lots of questions, and they will be happy to answer your own. Puppy mill owners will take money from anybody. Most conscientious breeders will offer you a contract that contains provisions about the puppy's health and temperament, and they will agree to take back a puppy that is not satisfactory.

A good breeder will, as breeder Georgia Parker points out, "mention the words spay or neuter" within five minutes of meeting you. Generally, a prospective buyer will sign a spay/neuter clause, unless the puppy is specifically intended to be shown.

Most reputable breeders don't advertise in newspapers—they already have enough prospective customers; in fact, they usually have a waiting list.

This doesn't mean that you can't get a good puppy from your neighbors or even from your second cousin. It does mean that you're taking a chance, not only with your money, but with your heart. Don't risk it; buy a healthy, well-bred Basset from someone who knows what he's doing.

Still, some remarkable Bassets have been rescued from pet stores, and even puppy mills. Here's one of my favorite stories, told by Karen Fetter:

> My Jake was a pet store Basset. He was five months old and being kept in a cage at the pet store. The management discounted him from $500.00 to $250.00. The shop told me he was howling all the time and they wished I would take him. I paid the money and brought him home that day. He was so weak from being in a cage so long that he couldn't even walk up a small hill near our house. One of our local vets said it was because of hip dysplasia and took x-rays. I took this set of x-rays to the pet store and demanded my money back. I got it—and kept the dog. Later on, additional x-rays showed that Jake was perfectly normal. So it turned out that Jake paid for himself, the pet shop got stuck, and I got a wonderful Basset Hound. He is now a healthy, happy guy able to run up hills and I love him dearly—no matter where he came from!

If you decide to buy from a breeder, be sure you get a pedigree that goes back **at least** three generations (five is better), a registration application or certificate, a sales contract, a veterinary record, and care instructions, such as what kind of food your puppy has been eating and so on.

I got my Basset from the pound. It seems like they always have a lot of Bassets there. Why?

Unfortunately, Basset acquisition (by one of us—the good guys) is all too often coupled with Basset dumping (by one of them—the bad guys). Not only Bassets, of course, but many wonderful pets end their days at the pound or animal shelter. The number of Bassets does seem large, however, considering that the breed is not one of the most common. Here are some reasons, given by the dumpers:

1. "I didn't know he was going to get this big."
2. "We bought him for the kids, but they're not interested in him anymore."
3. "He's too hard to housebreak."
4. "He barks all the time."
5. "He chews stuff."
6. "He keeps wandering off and we have to go get him."
7. "He needs surgery and we can't afford it."
8. "He's too old."
9. "He's too much trouble."

Appalling as these "reasons" appear to a responsible owner, they are the common ones. Unbelievably, people will deposit their aged Basset (whom they may have had for 10 years or more) with the pound, under the delusion that some happy couple will show up to adopt him. Fortunately, that does happen sometimes. It happened with our Miles and Ruby, with Mr. Mumbles and Chelsea, and with many others. But pets are abused, neglected, and euthanized by the millions in this country every year, simply because they are too much trouble. I won't tell any horror stories in this book, but there are plenty of them, and if you want to find out firsthand, go to your local animal shelter. Adopt a Basset or two while you're there, as well as a couple of cats.

But only do so if you are ready to commit yourself for the long haul—physically, emotionally, spiritually, and financially. Dogs are the most thoroughly domesticated of all animals; they have come a very long way from their ancestors, the wolves. Bassets have come a longer way than most, having almost no remnant of their wolfish pedigree (with the exception of their tendency to gather in packs and their beautiful atavistic howl).

No matter how independent and self-sufficient your Basset may appear, however, remember it's only an act—and a pretty bad one at that. Your hound is totally, one hundred percent dependent upon you for his food, shelter, and emotional well-being. Without your love and care, he will not survive, and that's a fact.

If, for reasons beyond your control, you must part with your beloved friend, seek the services of your nearest Basset Rescue Organization (there's a list at the back of the book, or the American Kennel Club can help direct you). These heroic folks will do their best to see that your Basset is placed in a loving and permanent adoptive home. If you are honest about any personality and health problems that the dog may have, your chances of getting him well-placed are increased. Some foster and adoptive parents take on ill, disabled, or temperamental Bassets as a special challenge.

Male or female?

Rumor has it that female dogs have sweeter, more dependent dispositions. I'm not sure about this. Both my friendliest and unfriendliest dogs have been male. If there is any truth to this generalization, however, it's well to remember that it **is** just that—a generalization. It's pretty well established that females are easier to housetrain (not easy mind you—just easier), and if you'd like two Bassets, a pair of females will bond better than a pair of males. Even better, as a rule, is to get a dog of each sex. Females are supposed to be less subject to roaming than males, but a responsible owner should never have to find this out the hard way.

Male dogs tend to be more territorial, a disposition sometimes unfortunately displayed by "marking" the household furniture. Females will not do this. They'll just go on the floor.

Luckily, Basset Hounds are not particularly territorial; after all, they're not Rottweilers. Male dogs also tend to be larger than the females—although one of the biggest Bassets I ever knew was of the feminine persuasion. It's also my firm conviction that male Basset Hounds are awful cowards, especially about things like nail trimming and baths. Just like men in general.

Puppy or adult?

Another major decision you may need to make (unless it has already been made for you) is whether to take a puppy or an adult dog. It may cheer you up to realize that pitfalls await you in either case. The advantage of getting a puppy consists primarily in the belief that such a young dog will bond with you and your family more easily. Bassets are not one-person dogs to begin with, however, and a dog of any age is likely to fit right in, so long as comfortable sleeping arrangements and plenty of food are provided. Those seem to be the main requirements, at least from the dog's point of view.

Another advantage: Puppies do not come with long histories of bad habits. (They have plenty of bad habits, of course, but they're **new** bad habits, which we all like to think of as somehow better than old bad habits.) And, of course, they are the cutest creatures imaginable, all paws and ears and deep, deep eyes. This may not make up for the fact that in getting a puppy, you have about four months of housetraining stretching before you. Remember that Bassets are much harder to housetrain than most dogs. Be prepared for the long haul. It's not unusual to have dogs of six months or even a year not completely trustworthy in the home (see Chapter 5).

If you are considering a puppy, try to meet both parents, if at all possible. Although the stud dog may not be on the premises, you should be able see photographs and get information about him. Sometimes people take it for granted that having both parents on hand is a good thing. All it means is that the stud fee was nonexistent. A responsible breeder will choose the best stud, and the best stud is probably not the dog who just happens to live in the house or to belong to the breeder's brother-in-law.

Do not take a puppy that looks ill or depressed. This may seem like common sense, but it is amazing how many people will select just this puppy, out of pity. This can turn out to be a very expensive and possibly fatal error.

Most puppies are taken from their mothers and sold when they are too young. Eight weeks is too early. Ten weeks is borderline. Twelve weeks is best. The puppies need the extra time after they are weaned to play actively with their littermates and become properly socialized with other dogs.

Socialization among dogs is not exactly what it is among humankind. Dogs do not live in a democratic society. They like order, and they like hierarchy. In a litter, one pup will be the "alpha," or top dog. While this may bother our democratic sense of justice, dogs don't seem to mind it a bit. More important for most of them is the issue of where they stand in the "pecking order." They just want to have a secure place in it somewhere. Bassets aren't interested in larger, metaphysical issues.

Trouble occurs when two or more dogs, unsure of their place, vie for the top position. This is where socializing experience within the litter can be helpful. But dogs taken out too soon may be insufficiently socialized and have difficulty detecting the signals that indicate litter position. They are lost, as it were, with no signposts.

Many aggressive dogs' problems can be traced to being taken too early from their litters. When dogs play together, they play-bite. (The technical name for this is "inhibited bite," which means they keep themselves from biting too hard.) This inhibited bite is one way top dogs reinforce their superior positions. But dogs taken away from the litter too soon may not understand how to play-bite. Their nips can turn into the real thing frighteningly fast. Never allow your puppy to nip you or your clothing. (Those 28 little baby teeth are sharp as razors, for one thing. Later on, your Basset will have 42 bigger but duller teeth.) In fact, never allow

A Basset puppy should not be taken from his litter until he's 12 weeks old. (Shelby, Tim and Janet Heald)

your puppy to do anything when he's young that you wouldn't want him to do when he's a great big Basset Hound!

My foster dog, Flash, had an uncontrolled aggression problem probably resulting from a combination of inbreeding and being removed from the litter too early. In two separate incidents, he attacked my other dogs' ears during play—badly enough to send them both to the vet for stitches. He actually bit large chunks off! Mugwump's ear looked like someone had taken a bite out of a slice of cheese. One of the saddest decisions I had to make was to put Flash down, but his biting habits had become dangerous to people as well as to our other pets. I sadly thank everyone who helped us through this difficult decision and painful time.

The biggest drawback to acquiring an adult dog is that many of them are given up for a reason! If the dog was abused or of poor breeding, he may be aggressive. He may have serious health or personality problems. For these and other reasons, it is best not to acquire your dog from a newspaper ad—the "Free to good home" type. This kind of pet is known as O.R. for "Owner Relinquished" and is another name for "trouble." You have no idea what kind of problems you're inheriting, or if the owner will suddenly decide that he wants his former pet back.

Get your adult dog from a reputable breeder, the Humane Society, or your local Basset rescue. These people are responsible and will tell you in advance about any personality quirks or health problems the dog may have. Reputable breeders can be located by contacting the Basset Hound Club of America (BHCA), which will then direct you to your local chapter. They will be happy to supply you with names and suggestions. Do not rush to the newspaper; what you'll almost certainly find listed are "backyard breeders" with little knowledge or experience about the breed.

Try to find out as much as possible about the dog's history: How many homes has he had, and why was he given away? Sometimes it may be because of a habit you may or may not be able to break or live with, such as incessant barking or housetraining mistakes. However, if you see the word "aggression" anywhere in the dog's case history, beware. Unless you are trained and willing to deal with an aggressive dog, you should avoid taking him.

Adopting a dog

When you receive a dog from a rescue organization or animal shelter, you will sign "adoption papers," which make the dog legally yours and spell out your financial and moral obligations to the animal. The adoption papers may also set up living standards for your dog and may involve a "home visit" before the adoption can be approved. Some people regard this as intrusive, but they shouldn't. This is all done to make sure that the new owner and dog will make a good, permanent "fit." No one wants to see the dog back in the shelter or in yet another foster home. No one wants to see children upset because their new pet is going away.

It would be unusual if your adopted pet had no problems. If he's from a shelter, the trauma of having been confined in a cage among a bunch of other strange dogs may make him depressed or frightened. If he was deposited in the shelter by people to whom he was attached, he may be grieving. A dog from a foster home may suffer the same separation anxiety and may take some extra time and patience to bond with you. Don't worry, it's worth it. Whether it's a new puppy or an older dog, sit down with your choice for a while before deciding. Remember, this will be a lifelong companion! Still, you may have your new pet "thrust upon you," as it were, and it's amazing how well this may work out.

This brings me to another, related point. Do not get a Basset Hound on impulse. Although we may have obeyed the instincts of our hearts on occasion, it's usually better to reflect and ask yourself some hard questions first.

Can you afford to keep a dog? Vet care is becoming increasingly expensive, not because the vets are gouging the owners, but because today we can treat illnesses that formerly we just had to suffer through. Heartworm pills, vaccinations, dental care, and other procedures are now the norm and are necessary for your dog's health. Puppies need vaccinations for canine distemper, canine viral hepatitis, canine leptospirosis, canine parvovirus, and rabies.

Once you get your dog home, you may have to introduce him to your established pets. If you have a cat, make sure the Basset and kitty are introduced to each other gradually. Bassets and cats make the best of pals, but cats are conservative in nature and need time to warm up to the slobbering monstrosity you have dragged in to their castle. If you own another dog, especially one of the same sex, there's a chance that some fighting may occur for the top spot. Keep each dog on a leash, and try to introduce them in a neutral spot—not the kitchen! Your first dog will probably be the alpha dog in the new arrangement, an outcome you should encourage but cannot force.

Never leave your pets alone together until you are sure they are friends. One method is the old sleep-together test. Once you see them snuggled up happily together, you can be pretty sure they are bonded. On the other hand, lots of dogs never sleep together, but remain on good terms all their lives. Still, it may be that your dogs will never grow to really like each other. Our rescue dog, Ruby, is not fond of ANY other dogs. She tolerates the others (barely) as long as they don't get too close. If you want to make sure your pets get along, you may want to try them out together first at the shelter or foster home.

Until your dogs are sleeping together, keep an eye out to make sure they're getting along. (Annabelle and Ruggie, Donna Caraway)

When you adopt a dog, you are promising to care for him to the best of your ability. And it may not be cheap.

Will you be able to provide the dog with a safe environment? This means a fenced-in yard, a yard that is not drenched in fertilizer (which can be dangerous to your pet), or a yard that is not loaded with deadly flora, such as Japanese yew. It is not, by the way, good enough to keep your dog on a chain or stake-out. These devices may be all right for temporary use, but they are hard on your Basset's neck and tend to promote territoriality and even viciousness. Don't use them.

If your dog has the run of the yard, be sure you keep the yard clean of feces. The number of flies that dog droppings can attract is amazing, and flies are not healthy for you or your pet. If one dog eats another's feces (sad to say, this is not unknown in the Basset world), he can acquire coccidia, little creatures that infest the intestinal tract and cause bloating and diarrhea. This infestation is not hard to treat, but you don't want your Basset to have the experience to begin with.

By the way, if you feed your dog a diet high in animal, as opposed to vegetable, protein, you find fewer little treasures to pick up. This is because animal protein is easier to digest than the vegetable kind; it is a more efficient food.

Safe environments also include no access to swimming pools. Remember, Basset Hounds are not Labradors. Although most can swim, and a few even enjoy it, they're just not very good at it.

If you leave your dog outside while you are gone, he should have direct access to the house or to a warm, dry shelter of his own. Check your Basset's bedding regularly to make sure it is dry, and be sure to wash it frequently. Not that Bassets are especially sensitive to dirt—in fact, they rather glory in it—but unwashed bedding harbors fleas. Indeed, fleas love to lay their eggs in dog bedding so that the young fleas, as they emerge, can be sure of a good supply of Basset blood right away.

Many dogs are terrified of thunder and should not be left outside when there is danger of a storm. Your Basset needs plenty of cool water to drink whether indoors or out, of course. Never deprive a dog of water because you are afraid he may wet on the carpet. Dedicated Basset owners often take their carpets up. It's easier that way, in the long run.

Will your Basset have enough of your company? Little makes me sadder than the thought of dogs being left alone hour after hour, day after day. They are by nature pack animals, and you are the pack leader. They don't always need to be doing something exciting (although a walk around the block is tremendously thrilling to a Basset), but they do like you to be with them. In fact, they like to be with you all the time, even—or especially— when you're in the bathroom.

Okay, everyone knows that you have to work, and most places of employment are curiously dog-unfriendly. So you can't bring your best pal with you. But the answer is not sticking him in a crate for 12 hours. Your dog is not an object, but a living being, who needs stimulation and exercise. You have several makeshift options. You can give your dog the run of the house, or a portion of it. You can (and should) give him a companion. You can ask a neighbor or pet sitter to come by and play with your dog or take him out for a walk. A dog lying alone all day in a house is not a happy dog.

If you must leave your dog alone, be sure to block off stairs and other hazards. Bassets, especially Basset puppies, aren't very good at navigating them. Baby gates are useful for this sort of thing, but a determined Basset can knock them over or even chew them to pieces. It's happened.

Chewing on baby gates is bad enough, but if your Basset starts chewing on electrical cords, there can be real trouble. Keep electrical cords out of the way! Again, this is a more likely hazard with puppies. It may sound silly, but crawling around your house at Basset height may alert you to problems you didn't notice before.

Provide your lonely dog with toys. It's best to have a suitable variety of them. I switch toys around, putting one away for a while, then bringing it down to the great delight of Ruby, who adores toys, especially the squeaky kind. Toys have advanced far beyond the simple squeak-squeak sort. Squeaky toys giggle, baa, croak, whine, snort, and gurgle. One company makes a roll-around toy in which a dog biscuit is hidden, thus keeping the dog fascinated, but tortured.

When you are away, it's best to keep on a radio, (with no upsetting talk shows). Bassets like elevator music best. If you can keep the house dim (not dark), your Basset may be encouraged to snooze away the lonely hours you'll be gone. It's worth a try.

Cabinets need to be closed, and in some cases locked. Bassets have been known to shove their noses right into handles and open said cabinets. If you do have ground-level cabinets, you can keep the onions there. Even Bassets won't eat onions.

When you are home, try giving your pet some "quality time," a nice long walk in a new place. Play with your dog, or work with him. (If you're doing this right, he won't know the difference.) I heard of a case where the owner crated the dog for 12 to 15 hours a day while she was at school, then came home and gave the dog a sedative so she wouldn't bark or play! Happily, the dog was given to Ohio Basset Rescue, which promptly found the animal a home with a young cancer patient, who had always longed for a Basset. Perhaps, as Rodica Stoicoiu says, they can heal each other.

Obtaining the Basset Hound, however, is only the first step in a lifetime of adventure. A typical day with a Basset was summed up by my friend, Shellie Smith:

> I spent the weekend alone with Fern. I had been looking forward to some "bonding" time with her as I had been on a business trip during most of the previous week. Hah! Some bonding! She's lucky I didn't bond her to the wall with duct tape. I was cleaning the upstairs rooms and was preparing to empty the cat litter when Fernie decided to poke her head in for a feast. I yelled and she withdrew her head and stalked off. Minutes later, she returned to the room with a mouthful of toilet paper from the bathroom. I yelled again. She spit out the paper and repeated the stalking act. Wary this time, I picked up the paper and turned around just in time to see her squat and pee right on the floor, and five feet from where I was standing! Hoarse by this time, I put her outside on the cable for a few minutes while I cleaned up the mess.

> Tired now, I let her in and sat on the sofa with a cookie. Just at this time, I heard Steve come home and I put the cookie on top of the table out of her reach (yes, you know what's coming). Together we went into the kitchen to greet Steve. Fern was wild with joy, since he'd been gone for two days. Suddenly, she darted out of the room. We both stood there, puzzled, until I remembered the cookie. So much for being the superior species, huh? I raced into the living room and had to pry open her jaws to

Fern was up to every kind of Basset mischief in a single weekend.

remove the cookie, solid chocolate of course. What a weekend! She was so mad at me she wouldn't come to bed. At 1:30 A.M. I woke up and caught her devouring an empty pizza box she'd knocked down from the stove. She had a crust hanging from her mouth like a cigarette. I need a weekend to relax from the weekend.

Routine care of Bassets often inspires owners to what some might consider rather eccentric behavior. For example, Jeanne McBride sings to her dog, Cleo, but she has a reason:

I admit I sing to Cleo, but I use it as a training device. We play "This Little Piggy" with her feet, and end up in belly rubs. (This is a fun way to get her used to my handling her toes for nail clipping.) I also hold her ears out and sing "The Flying Nun" theme song. (This helps air out her ears and gets her used to my handling them.) We also do "I'm a Little Teapot" where I use her snout as the spout, so she knows it's all right for me to handle her nose. My singing, as bad as it is, makes her happy.

That's another great thing about Bassets—they are such an uncritical audience.

Basset owners often go to lengths others may find incomprehensible. To most of us, however, it makes perfect sense. For example, Susan Hurt writes:

Now I truly realize where my priorities are—with my Basset. I live in an apartment and have always been reluctant to consider a house because of the hassle involved. But today I toured a house for sale that overlooks the Missouri River. I think Perdita would like to live in this house, as it has four bedrooms and I'd give one of them to her. She would have three beautiful, scenic acres over which to roam, a deck off the kitchen, and a huge basement. I think Perdita would like the house very much. Maybe we will buy it, even though it is quite expensive. I see myself at night, overlooking the Missouri River, my dog in my arms—what bliss!

To which Karen Fetter responds:

The house you looked at sounds wonderful. If Perdita doesn't like the setup, let me know. Jake and I are very flexible.

What names do owners choose for Bassets?

I think that the choice of a name is one of the most critical decisions. In important ways, it defines the whole relationship. It also affects the entire course of a dog's career. Let me illustrate with a case from my own experience. Bubba was my first foster dog. He came to me with the name of Bubba. Right away, I knew Bubba needed to reinvent himself. With a name like Bubba hanging over his head, it seemed as if he might be capable of anything low or trashy. So I renamed him. I gave him the serene, noble, and, most important—considering Bubba's level of intellect—simple name of Bob. Now the whole time Bob resided with me, I had no problems whatsoever with him. He lived a simple and dignified life. He lived up to his name. Eventually Bob was adopted by a loving and caring owner, who decided to reinstate his original name. Needless to say, a dog named Bubba begins to act like a dog named Bubba. Although things worked out well in the end, let me just say that in my opinion only, Bob would have been better off as Bob.

John Warner calls his Basset Ruby, a name that can be carried on the wind!

For some reason, names associated with the immortal detective Sherlock Holmes are very popular, although to my knowledge, Mr. Holmes suffered a Bassetless existence. Holmes, Moriarty, Sherlock, Watson, and Mrs. Hudson are all fine names. Most dog owners nowadays seem to give their dogs people names. You don't see any Rovers or Fidos anymore. (President Lincoln owned a Fido, but, unfortunately, it was not a Basset.) Millie, Max, Annie, Sadie, Fred, Barney, and the like are popular. So are surnames like Wilson, Barkley, and Kramer. A few people name their hounds after distinguishing marks, such as Freckles, Wrinkles, or Spots.

Try to choose a name that sounds good when you're yelling it all around the neighborhood. We made this mistake with Mugwump and Miles. These names just don't holler well. Ruby, however, is a name that can be carried on the wind.

Not that it makes a whole lot of difference whether the name carries on the wind or not. The chances are that your Basset Hound won't come anyway.

The most important consideration about naming your Basset Hound should be "Does the name fit the dog?" Never pick out a name in advance—it should come spontaneously, preferably in a mystical vision, or at least after a great party. Then check to see if it still sounds good when you're sober. Does the name look like your Basset? Naming your Basset after a deceased great uncle is also a nice touch. I recommend it.

THREE

The Beauty of the Beast, or Is There Something Wrong with That Dog? It Looks Awful!

The Basset Hound is a dwarf breed, which may account for its expression, which often appears to be sad. It is an error, though, to think Bassets always appear so miserable. They can also look doleful, lugubrious, mournful, glum, gloomy, morose, sober, somber, forlorn, sorrowful, and melancholy. When they really lighten up, they can become positively pensive. I've heard the Basset described as having a "rather medieval appearance," and I guess that about sums it up. There wasn't much to laugh about in the Dark Ages.

The word "basset" simply means "low" in French, and the adjective is often applied to various dogs that are "lower" than others of their general breed type. (Some Basset owners claim that their dogs are low in more ways than one.)

As mentioned in Chapter 1, Bassets come in several varieties—both smooth and rough coated, crooked and straight legged. In addition to our own familiar (what I call "classic") Basset, there are the Basset Artesien Normand (or Basset d'Artois), which is similar to, but smaller than, the "classic" Basset; and the Basset Fauve de Bretagne (a cross between the Grand Griffon Fauve de Bretagne and the Basset Vendeen, if that clears up anything for you). In the pictures I have seen of this animal, it looks slightly shaggy and somewhat terrier-like. Apparently, it also possesses the rather snippety, sharp, and difficult terrier personality. The Basset Griffon Vendeen (rough or wire coated) is itself a cross between the white St. Hubert, the white and tan Italian Hound, and the "King's White" Grand Griffon. There is also a very fine looking Basset Bleu de Gascogne. These sorts of Bassets have evolved through the ages, and in France, for example, the rough-coated sort are more popular than the smooth. The rough coat and longer legs, by the way, are recessive traits that may crop up from time to time in the "classic" Basset. In fact, there are a few longer-legged Bassets used for hunting purposes even in the United States.

Now that we have mentioned all these variants, we'll do our best to forget about them and talk about the classic American Basset Hound. Let's look at what the breed standard of the American Kennel Club says a Basset ought to look like. The breed standard is the criterion by which all Basset Hounds are measured in the show ring (although not in the hearts of those of us who have less than perfect models).

Any hound color is acceptable, and no preference is given to one shade over another, although all of us have our little partialities, I suppose. Anyway, Bassets can range from true black (very unusual) through reds and brown to the unearthly "lemon" Basset, a very pale, cream-colored beauty. Most common is the classical tricolor Basset, followed by the red and white. Occasionally, one hears of a blue Basset, but this condition is due to a genetic defect and is distinctly undesirable. The Basset coat, whatever the color, should be hard and shiny, with a beautiful luster. One of the sneakiest things about Basset Hounds is that their color can change from puppyhood to adulthood. Many pups that are almost pure white when born get attacked by the "freckle fairy" and develop little spots. Officially, this is known as "ticking," but I prefer the freckle fairy concept.

Another sneaky thing about Basset Hounds is how much they weigh, which is always a lot more than you think. Even a medium-weight Basset weighs about 45 pounds, and some have been known to tip (or crash) the scales at nearly 100 pounds. The reason for the discrepancy between looks

Zach, Gretchen Laffert

and actual weight is partly due to the Basset's unusual bone density. Recall that the Basset is a dwarf breed, which means that his bone structure is similar to that of a Bloodhound or other large, heavy dog. The old adage that a Basset Hound is a very large dog on very short legs is quite true. And "short" is the key. Bassets should measure between 11 and 14 inches at the highest point of the shoulder. Over 15 inches means disqualification from events that require adherence to the breed standard. Males, by the way, tend to be noticeably larger than females. They also drool more.

The breed standard was developed so that both ordinary people and show ring judges can tell the superior Basset from the mediocre one, although I must say that my few forays into dog showdom have made me wonder if the judges have a secret standard to which they refer without telling the rest of us. For example, the breed standard says, plainly enough, "Being a scenting dog with short legs, it holds its nose low to the ground." Now that makes sense. Tracking rabbits and so forth requires one to keep one's nose to the grindstone, as it were. At the shows I attended, however, I was particularly struck with the way the handlers kept yanking (I'm afraid that's the only word for it) at the dog's neck to make it trot along with the head **up** rather than naturally low. Well, I'm no expert, of course. The handlers obviously knew what they were doing, since ribbons and trophies were handed round without anyone but me mentioning this little discrepancy between the breed standard and actual practice.

Back to the breed standard. I'm reading the part about gait, which refers to the way the Basset should move. The standard says, "The Basset Hound moves in a smooth, powerful, and effortless manner." Check out your Basset and see if this applies. I think the word "waddle" more accurately describes the way my dog, Mugwump, ambulates, although she can be surprisingly fast on escape. At this point, her waddle evolves rather rapidly into a "lumber." The standard continues, "Its gait is absolutely true with perfect coordination between the front and hind legs." I like that part. I suppose it's fairly true to say that if the dog did not move with "perfect coordination between the front and hind legs," it would fall down, and we certainly don't want that happening.

Bassets always seem to weigh a lot more than you think.

"The tail should be carried merrily aloft" (actually, the standard says "gaily," but I changed it). The Basset, therefore, has a gradually rising appearance—from the nose buried in the dirt seeking treasure, to the smooth sweep of the (I hope) straight and unsagging back, and up along the joyful curve of the tail into the pure blue sky. If the classical picture of a Basset looks nothing like your own precious pet, no matter. Enjoy him anyway.

Skipping around the breed standard, I come to the head, which, the standard informs me, should not be "dry." Now I think I know what the word "dry" means, but in my book, it's kind of a temporary condition—the opposite of wet. Betting it meant something else deep in Bassetdom, I asked a few people when I was at the show. Dry means not wrinkled, they told me, and the Basset's head, ideally, should be a positive mass of wrinkles, as though it really belonged to some other, bigger dog. Therefore, it shouldn't be dry. This sort of makes sense, but I keep wondering why the standard simply doesn't say that the face should be wrinkled. Just for fun, I checked my Webster's Ninth New Collegiate Dictionary (published quite a while after the breed standard was accepted in 1964), and although the entry "dry" provided me with 16 definitions, none of them had anything to do with wrinkles. C'est le Basset.

The ears should be extremely long, so long that they come well beyond the tip of the nose when pulled gently forward. Long ears are the sine qua non of the Basset Hound, along with its massive paws and wrinkled skin. As Shakespeare wrote, they should "sweep away the morning dew."

The legs, of course, should be crooked. This can be a surprise, by the way, even to veterinarians who are unfamiliar with the breed, and even to some who are. When I brought Miles in for an X-ray once, the vet, staring at the radiograph, said, "That's the problem with Bassets. Look at the way that bone is bent." "Doctor," I said gently, "the X-ray is upside down."

Patty Nordstrom's Basset, Smuckers, has the desirable extremely long ears.

I had to admit, though, that it didn't look any better right-side up. As Jerry Evenden, of Basset-L, commented, "A vet with the National Institute of Health commented to my wife: 'A Basset's bone structure looks like a bad accident.'" And remember, that's the breed standard.

Let's think about this. We basseteers are intoxicated with a breed whose distinguishing characteristics are dwarfism, big feet, drooping ears, wrinkled skin, and a miserable expression. We're special.

Bassets may have big feet, drooping ears, wrinkled skin, and miserable expressions, but they are still irresistible. (Maggie, Nancy Pelley)

Personality (Weird) and Habits (Beastly)

"Living with a Basset is like living with a very short clown."

—Anne Whitacre

My Basset seems lazy. Is this normal?

Although a dwarf breed, the Basset Hound has inherited none of the Seven Dwarves' work ethic. "Hi Ho, Hi Ho, it's off to work we go!" is definitely not the Basset Hound's motto. (JoAnne Smith has a sign that says, "Warning! Don't trip over the guard dog!")

Actually, Bassets make quite an effort to achieve the desired degree of total laziness. They have, over time, evolved many positions for total relaxation. Amy Zaremski has provided us with an analysis of several:

Frog or turkey leg: On stomach, legs sticking out in back.

Belly flop: On stomach, legs tucked under.

Royal raised head: Identical to the classic belly flop, except head conveniently elevated, resting on arm of arm chair, couch, or human leg.

37

Dallas Alice, who belongs to Donna Matushak-Funk, demonstrates the frog or turkey leg pose, good for total relaxation.

Corkscrew: On stomach, head to side opposite back feet.

Dead dog: Flat out on side.

Winter ball: Curled up, preferably on the couch, tail covering nose.

Classic back: Totally relaxed, fully on back, ready for a belly rub.

On the other hand, Bassets can be deceiving in this regard. While watching an escaped Basset charge happily around the ring in an obedience class, the bewildered judge remarked: "I didn't think Bassets could move that fast." One of the great wonders of the Basset world, in fact, is the dexterity with which a slovenly, fat, couch potato Basset can turn into a lean, mean escape machine.

They're stubborn, too. Patty Nordstrom needs to exercise a few pounds off her Basset, Smuckers. Smuckers is not as cooperative as she might be. Patty writes:

> In the evening we start out and everything is okay, but after about 10 minutes, she plants all four legs and refuses to move unless it is in the direction of home. If I can get my husband to walk with us, she does better, and if I can get her best friend, Dominique, a white boxer, to come, she will walk until her legs fall off. Any suggestions?

It looks to me like Patty needs an additional Basset, one that will give Smuckers a run for it.

Smuckers prefers a snooze to exercise.

Along with the Basset's famed laziness is a related characteristic: stubbornness, generally evinced by NOT wanting to move, or as we say in Basset circles, ground hugging. JoAnne Smith writes:

> We've found with our Bassets, especially Katsie, that when they don't want to move, they increase their body weight by about 1.5 tons and little suction cups come out of their front paws, enabling them to glue themselves to the ground. If you have one person tug from the front and one push from the back, all that will happen is that their back end goes up in the air and they kind of stand on their heads. This happens a lot on the way to the bathtub.

Karl Heege calls this behavior "throwing the anchor" and explains:

> When Watson throws the anchor on our walks, he looks like roadkill. Then, when you come up to him to prod, coax, plead, and beg to get him to move on, he does what any true Basset does: he rolls onto his back for a belly rub. It has become quite a game with him. When he

does his "dead dog" routine, I revive him with a few pumps on his chest—the closest thing he's going to get to a belly rub while on a walk. He then springs to his feet and away we go!

Basset laziness can be a community problem. John Grogan tells us that when he was younger, his family had to drive along some hilly roads in upstate New York to reach the family cabin. He remarks:

> At one particular curve, there was about a 2 in 10 chance of rounding the corner and finding a Basset Hound in the road—sunning himself on the double yellow lines. The general procedure was to stop the car, wait for a while, and then begin honking the horn. After about 30 seconds of honking, the Basset would turn his droopy eyes toward the car. He was clearly perturbed that someone was disturbing his nap. Then, with an almost audible harrumph, he would get up and waddle to the side of the road.

Although Diane Morgan's dog, Bob, hasn't placed himself in the middle of a busy road, he is clearly unconcerned about where he rests his weary head.

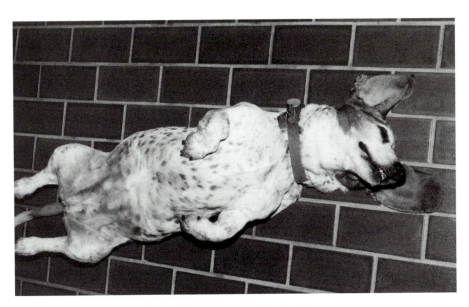

The essence of Basset laziness: Mercedes owned by Jan Green.

Some Bassets manage to combine energy and stubbornness in a novel and embarrassing way. Jerry Evenden writes:

I normally give Katie a morning walk of two or three hours duration, which covers about three miles. Regardless of our routes, Katie seems able to determine when we are heading home and starts a wide variety of delaying tactics to extend the walk period.

This morning, when we were about three-quarters of a mile from home, we had to cross a moderately busy intersection that had well-marked crosswalks painted with a solid yellow center and white border stripes. As we were crossing the street, I noticed a slightly greater than usual resistance. I turned to find Katie lying on her back in the middle of the street, feet spread out to the four compass points as if she was expecting a belly rub, tongue hanging out, and big grin on her face as I was "dragging" her across the street on her back. The layers of yellow paint had made the crosswalk so slick it was like sliding her across a newly waxed floor.

Of course this made it look like a case of felony animal abuse; I kept waiting for the SPCA enforcement officer to appear anytime.

Why does my Basset roam?

Bassets are hounds, and it is the very nature of the hound, especially the scent hound, to roam. (Many are lazy roamers, however; they sort of slide away while you're not looking.) They were designed to follow their noses wherever they lead, which may include snake-ridden swamps, skunk hideaways, the neighbor's trash, and rush-hour traffic. Bassets, clever creatures that they are, can combine the utmost laziness with a passion for seeing— or in their case, smelling—the world. The trouble they get into around the house is often a direct result of their thwarted wanderlust.

Although it is certainly possible that your Basset may come home from his forays unscathed, he, like your congressman, is not likely to have made the world a better place for his junket. It is far better that he stay at home. Gretchen Laffert writes:

> *Wandering souls. I take my dogs off leash a lot. They are unusual and do stay with me, but I NEVER take my eyes off them. They never run away, just walk off sniffing every blade of grass. It is never a good idea to let your Basset out alone and expect it to stay in the yard on its own honor.*

In general, a safe Basset is a fenced-in Basset. It is not sufficient to own several acres and have the hound run around loose. He will soon run off (being a hound), and very soon after that he will get into trouble (being a Basset). He may be killed by a car, a bullet, a rock, a Pit Bull, a poisonous delectable, and so on. You wouldn't allow your two-year-old child to wander around unsupervised; don't allow your dog to do so either.

Even if your yard is fenced, some Bassets can dig their way out. Hounds as a rule are **very** good diggers. Run a board along the bottom portion of the fence to prevent this from happening. Some people report excellent results with "invisible" fencing. I don't recommend this myself—it doesn't keep any dog or a small child out of your yard, for instance. You also have to replace batteries every six weeks or so, and it's possible you might forget to do so. Some Bassets, if strongly provoked (the mere sight or scent of a rabbit will do it), will run right through an electric fence. Then, too, some absent-minded member of the family is apt to turn off the fence without bothering to tell anyone. The next thing you know, your Basset is in the street, directly in the path of an oncoming car.

With the so-called "invisible" or electric fence, your dog must wear a special "wired collar," which is designed to give him a slight electrical shock if he strays too near the boundary. I don't like this idea.

In any fenced area, the danger zone is the gate. Make sure it fits snugly so that your dog can't get his head stuck between the gate and the fence. Some animals are also good at forcing gates open. We have to keep ours not only closed, but locked and tied.

Kathy Werley writes that Jeb, a Basset that belonged to her husband, Mitch, when he was boy, had a special twist to his wandering adventures:

> Jeb liked to wander out of the yard by learning how to get out of the gate. I don't know how he did it, but he did. Anyway, one day the cops picked him up when he was wandering around Kutztown, Pennsylvania. They knew him, of course. Everybody did. They proceeded to take him home, but when they arrived there, Jeb refused to leave the patrol car. (He even growled at my father-in-law, and then howled.) My father-in-law explained to the cops that there was no help for it but that they had to ride around town with the dog until Jeb was ready to return home. For some reason, known only to themselves, the police agreed that this was a perfectly reasonable thing to do, and for the next few hours, Jeb was the canine unit for Kutztown. At the end of the shift, Jeb was returned home without incident, spoiled and happy.

Karen Clemente's Ashley B. manages to combine roaming with laziness in a delicious way:

> Last week she managed to get out of the house and ran very quickly down the block, trailed by me and my husband screaming for her to stop. Did she listen? No-o-o. About three-quarters of a block farther on, she encountered a very nice man, who decided that the two idiots running and screaming far behind were her owners. He stopped her by giving her a belly rub. When we finally caught up to her, she looked at us as if to say, "Yes, this is worth it; I must do it again sometime soon." She licked the guy to thank him for her belly rub and off home she went, very proud of herself.

Karen Clemente's Ashley B. doesn't always look this angelic. Like other Bassets, she has a penchant for roaming.

Karen was lucky. Sometimes an escaped Basset will disappear—sometimes forever. Keep up-to-date color photos of your Basset in case the worst happens, and distribute them to your neighbors, local animal shelter, and every bulletin board you can find. Keep trying, and be an aggressive looker. Do not assume that the shelter will call you.

Then there is the tale of Cera's and Peabody's (who belong, at least in name, to Amanda Sherwin) Excellent Adventure. Peabody himself writes:

Wonder of Wonders! The back gate got left open today. Mom and Dad were inside, and we didn't want to bother them. Cera likes to go fast, so she raced out of the yard. I don't know where she went. I like to take my time and smell everything, and Mom walks too fast.

So today I got to go under the porch (Mom's mean about that) and sniff where the neighbor's cat comes to bother us. That took about 15 minutes, maybe 20. I like to do a thorough job. Then I wandered through Mom's herb garden, where she never lets me go. The dirt is really good for digging there. I also had time to check out the ivy bed, under the evergreens. [Note: See "Can Bassets Garden?" below.]

Then for the really fun part. I went across the road! The neighbor there has three cats and I've been anxious to meet them. Unfortunately, the neighbor wasn't around, and the cats weren't very friendly. But the garage was open and there was some good garbage, kinda mixed in with something Mom called tar.

Well, after about an hour, I heard Mom calling me. She sounded like she really wanted to see me, so I took my time. I still had a lot of garbage to finish, and I also wanted a walk down the road. By the time I got there, though, I saw Dad in the car. He opened the door and helped me get in. We found Cera, too, down the road. Boy, was Mom happy to see us! We got lots of cookies and stuff. I decided not to mention the garbage, but somehow Mom knew about it anyway. She also knew about the tar.

Cera and Peabody are a pair of wandering souls, when they're not in holiday garb. (Amanda Sherwin)

By the way, if your Basset gets into tar, the **only safe way to remove it** is by clipping it out. Do not use a solvent, which is likely to be poisonous, irritating to the dog's skin, and flammable. A bad combination.

Our Miles ran off after a wild goat one day, and we didn't find him until the next day, stretched out across the road. I thought he had been hit by a car. But no, he was only sleeping in the middle of the road, where there was plenty of room, apparently.

Anita Wright's rescue Basset, Watson, also has a tendency to wander. (In case you're wondering, a rescue Basset is not a hound with a brandy keg around his neck. It is one that has been "rescued" from the pound.) At any rate, Watson recently escaped from his yard, but he was found by a nice neighbor, who plied the Basset with ice cream cones as he played happily with the children. The neighbor phoned Anita saying, "he would baby-sit Watson anytime, as he is such a nice boy." We virtually had to drag him home. I felt quite put out that an ice cream cone could sway Watson's loyalty so easily. Still, I think he had made his living begging for a while before I got him, so maybe he thinks he has to keep in practice.

Anita may be putting too good a face on all this. As Jerry Evenden responded:

> I find Bassets to be total opportunists. They'll follow whoever gives them the treats. When I adopted Katie from her previous owner, she greeted me with kisses and gladly hopped into my car and never looked back. I'm sure this was not due to unkindness on the former owner's part, and I'm sure she would do the same if I gave her to someone else. She's just an affectionate lady who will camp wherever someone gives her attention.

The subject of wandering Bassets brings up an important point. Be sure that your Basset has identification at all times. Anything is better than nothing—from the old-fashioned dog tag dangling from the collar to the sewn-in name or nameplate on the collar to the tattoo (on the ear, inner hind leg, or belly) or flashy microchip between the shoulder blades.

One of the best ways to prevent the desire to wander (and the consequent hole-digging, howling, clothes-eating, house-destroying habits that go with it) is to give your hound plenty of exercise. Bassets are hunting dogs, after all! Jogs in the park, sturdy hikes through the foothills, or a dash to the grocery store all add spice to his life and strength to his bones. Don't expect your Basset to exercise himself in your yard, no matter how large it is. He already knows every bit of that yard. He has examined it inch by inch with his nose. He's eaten some of it. He's bored with it. Turn off the television, leave the dishes in the sink, and get yourself outside with your dog. Take him somewhere new, or at least somewhere he hasn't seen for a few days. You'll both be energized by the experience.

Are Bassets loyal?

GRACIE

Pam Posey-Tanzey

Bassets are not one-person dogs, thank heaven. They are family dogs and (contrary to Gracie's behavior) love everyone in the family. They are not apt to attack your guests, although many are somewhat aloof (or at least as aloof as a 14-inch being can be) with strangers. Until the stranger feeds him, of course. Then the stranger's part of the family.

Bassets are very loyal, according to Kathy Agel. "Davey sleeps on my side of the bed, follows me to the bathroom (he guards me while I take a shower in the morning), and will leave his dinner if I call." Kathy had to leave Davey for a weekend, and Davey suffered:

> While I was gone, he slept on my pillow, both day and night. He drove Bobby nuts, looking out the window to see if I was on my way home and crying when he didn't see me. When I finally did get home, he gave me the devil for being gone—then followed every step I took. He mumbled for several minutes before we went to sleep (he was in my arms as usual) and didn't jump down from the bed at all for the rest of the night. (He usually jumps down at least twice, and of course, he wakes me up for a boost back onto the mattress.) I couldn't go anywhere the next day without a 55-pound, red-and-white shadow. That's my boy!

Why does my Basset Hound race around the house barking like mad after he's just been outside in the yard or pen?

This seems to be a mystery, but about 88 percent of all Basset Hounds act like maniacs for about 15 minutes after being let into the house. They also do it after baths.

Some crazed folks, like ourselves, bark and howl along WITH our Bassets for the sheer joy of the thing.

Sue Lockhart, by the way, advises us NOT to shout at our Bassets to shut them up. They merely think we are joining in the fun. She remarks:

> When mine get going, I speak softly but carry a squirt bottle filled with cold water. A squirt in the face stops them instantly. Meanwhile you can talk to them pleasantly and tell them they're good when they stop.

This may work for Sue, but my Bassets aren't intimidated by any pleasant talking, let me tell you. They play for higher stakes, like food.

The best thing to do is to anticipate the mad dash around the breakfast table and put lamps and other breakables out of the path of the charging Basset. You might try distracting the beast with a dog biscuit, but the chances are that he'll gulp down the dog biscuit and then race away undeterred.

The 11.5 percent of Bassets who do not race madly around the house present their own challenge. These Bassets take the opposite tack. They lie down in the tub and won't get up. You can yell, jump up and down, and wave your arms, but there they stay, glaring balefully at you. They stay there for a long, long time, a wet soggy mass of Basset. They also clog up the drain.

Are Bassets good at interior decoration?

GRACIE

Pam Posey-Tanzey

GRACIE

Pam Posey-Tanzey

Bassets are adept at transforming the appearance of your home, although in some cases, innovative Basset tastes are at odds with the conventional ideas of beauty harbored by most owners. Alex Shapiro writes:

> One day, upon returning from school, I gave our former Basset, Sam, his tummy rub and then went to my room to rest. After about 20 minutes or so I became aware of a dark, eerie silence in the house. As all Basset owners know, this is the most dangerous signal a Basset can give that SOMETHING is going on. I went into the living room to check out the silence. Sure enough, Sam had gone and pulled another Bassetism. He had somehow gone to the cupboard and gotten out a bag of flour, which he had first played with and then spread all over the living room. It was beginning to look a lot like Christmas. Everything was covered with flour, including Sam's ears. To make it worse, Sam had gotten a drink of water after coating said ears in flour. His ears were now completely stiff

and ready to bake for 30 minutes at 450 degrees. [The flour had to be chipped off.]

Anne Whitacre's Esther has her own style:

Last week I came home to find that Esther had ripped open a seam in my arm chair cushion, and then carefully pulled the stuffing out in a long strand that stretched over the length of the living room and into the dining room. Then today, she took one of the bound books from a client of mine, carried it into the living room, and strewed all its 200 pages around the coffee table.

Bassets are a dangerous commodity when unshackled in the home. Suzanne Earley writes of her Emmett:

His big thing is that he knows how to open drawers and cupboards—of **all** kinds. He's figured out the knobs. He also opens zippers! When I had my overnight bag on the floor, he unzipped the bag, took out the toiletries bag inside, and then unzipped it too! He proceeded to root through the bag until he found my toothbrush, which is now covered with bite marks. He also loves people toothpaste and goes ballistic when he sees people brushing their teeth!

Advanced Bassets decorate using their various bodily products. I can't—and do not wish to—repeat the numerous tales involving clever Basset deposits of urine, vomit, and feces in many interesting and unexpected parts of the house. A less offensive story and question comes from Karen Conaway:

On the subject of dreaded DROOL—any suggestions on cleaning walls? I have scrubbed the paint off the wall in a couple of spots. I haven't found ANYTHING that will take it off. Annabelle seems to have an abundant supply of it. Help!

Basset drool is an amazing substance that defies chemical analysis. It cannot be removed. At least that's what I thought until Bill James, under force of grim necessity, did find a solution, literally:

Saturday night I dropped a full bag of stale marshmallows into the kitchen trash. When I arose on Sunday, Molly has just finished the bag.

Apparently, Basset Hound drool is a solvent for stale marshmallows. Molly had obviously enjoyed her treat. Her ears, face, chin, chest, and front legs were covered with a thick, sticky coating of dissolved marshmallow. So were the kitchen walls, ceilings, and floor. I used a paint-stripping solvent on those surfaces. Warm water will not remove marshmallow from Basset Hounds. Marshmallow slime throws back its head and laughs at several varieties of dog shampoo. And people shampoo. Eventually, I managed to remove most of it with Head and Shoulders Dandruff Shampoo. At least she doesn't stick to the floors any more.

Drool does, on the other hand, have some properties that might well be worth scientific investigation. From Kris and Hope Ebbert:

We had a sickly looking spider plant that just happened to be near Murphy's water and food dishes. Lately, whenever I change her water, I've been pouring the slimy remains into the plant. I don't know what substances Murphy has been drooling into her water dish, but this plant is now ENORMOUS! Next year, maybe we'll raise pumpkins. Using Basset drool, we should be able to grow a couple of thousand-pounders!

Fortunately or unfortunately, depending on the way you look at it, not all Bassets drool. There seems to be a direct relationship between Basset size and the amount of drool produced. In other words, the bigger the Basset, the more drool. This is because the bigger, heavier Bassets are endowed with bigger flews, those pendulous lips hanging on your Basset's face. Flews are drool collectors and when a sufficient amount of drool is collected, the Basset shakes his head and lets it fly. Voila!

Sudden drooling, by the way, might indicate a problem with your dog's teeth. Seek a professional opinion.

Can Bassets swim? Do they want to?

My dog, Miles, cannot swim. He can, however, work himself into a trance by staring Narcissus-like at his reflection in the swimming pool, after which he simply tumbles into the water and flounders around until someone comes to save him.

It's a fact that Bassets possess an uncanny, some say supernatural, knack for being able to find any pool of water within five square miles and thereupon falling into it and drowning. Bassets are not naturally expert swimmers like Newfoundlands or Labradors, and they should never be left unattended in a swimming area. Long bodies and short legs do not make for English Channel–type crossings. Your Basset will be lucky if he can make it across the pool. It's a good idea, though, to teach your Basset where the stairs to the pool are, so that if someone does leave the gate open and he falls in (like our Miles), he will at least be able to get out again.

JoAnne's Basset, Augustus, weighs 97 pounds. "And he's not fat," says JoAnne. "He's big, very big. When he tries to swim (and he likes water), he does okay as long as he's going in a straight line. When he tries to turn, he begins to sink—slowly, sort of like the *Titanic*. The last thing you see on his face is a 'What the ???' expression as he slowly submerges." JoAnne adds, "We don't take him swimming much, and when we do, it's in shallow water."

Alvaro Aguilar sums it up neatly:

> Not to discourage you, but Bassets are not made for water. With their short legs and heavy bodies, it's no wonder you don't see Basset adventure movies.

If you want to make your Basset feel really ridiculous, you might provide a wading pool for him, but it's a relatively rare hound who will deliberately get near water in any form (including sprinklers). All the water he needs can be provided via his drinking bowl. Make sure he gets plenty of it. You can throw a few ice cubes in it in the summertime to help keep it cool.

"I'm sure I dropped a bone in here . . . "

Bassets usually prefer the beach to the ocean. (Sophie, Jan Green)

Judy Trenck's Georgie spends most of her pool time chasing the lizards that congregate around the pool:

> One ran in the pool the other day; I threw it out, but Georgie kept looking in the pool. She walked the entire distance around the pool, ears dragging in the water, looking for the silly lizard.

Believe it or not, several companies manufacture life preservers for dogs, so if you are planning a little canoeing outing, it would be a good idea to stuff your dog into one of these rather ungainly devices for his own safety.

There is no way your Basset can keep from looking like a fool while wearing one of these things, so don't forget to take a picture of him for the family album. You can even put water wings on him.

Can Bassets garden?

Delightfully well. Ms. Molly Dog, canine companion of Bill James, otherwise known as The Bearded One (TBO), comments in her own inimitable voice:

> Bosley, our temporary dog, learned a new trick today, and TBO was not pleased. Los Angeles is enjoying 90 degree weather, and TBO went to the garden shop and bought some new flowers. We always have Iceland poppies and snapdragons growing in the garden during the winter. This gives TBO, who raves about his vegetable garden, but really hates vegetables, a chance to escape to the better culinary world of homemade chili dogs, fried chicken, and all that other artery clogging stuff.

"Looks like they need fertilizing to me." (Barney, Mitch and Kathy Werley)

After carefully digging up the remains of the summer corn crop, the crop that ClioPatra almost single-handedly ate, TBO carefully turned a couple hundred pounds of compost and soil conditioner into the raised garden. He then meticulously smoothed out the dirt and measured where each plant would go so as to present the most pleasing appearance. This always surprises Mrs. TBO who can't even get him to wear matching socks most of the time. Anyway, after the last snapdragon and poppy had been lovingly placed, each with a small handful of fertilizer to help them get started, Bosley went over the edge.

Now Bosley is still on thin ice for stealing TBO's cookie a few days ago, and this may seal the Temp's fate once and for all. As The Bearded One sat back with a glass of iced tea to survey his work, Bosley hopped into the raised planter. He very gingerly sniffed his way clear around the railroad tie edges. That was kind of cute. Suddenly he leapt into the middle of the garden, with a routine that would have made a truffle hound proud. He jammed his nose into about two inches of loamy soil and started to run, leaving a furrow as wide as his nose from one end of the garden to the other. He slowed a few times to snort out the dirt that rammed itself up his nostrils. By the time he was through, only two snapdragons were left standing. Bosley rolled over on them and asked for a tummy rub. His request was denied.

Against all odds, it seems, Bosley still resides with TBO.

Do Bassets have any special bedtime tricks?

Yes, but maybe not the kind you're thinking of. Bassets will go to any length to get out of their own proper dog beds and into bed with you, where they think they belong. I guess they feel they can protect you better from intruders or killers that way. Anita Wright describes her Mumbles's polished technique:

> Last night, my husband tucked Mumbles in, and when he asked him for a kiss, Mumbles just scowled at him. A really mean look. Terry got into bed and Mumbles got up and stood next to the bed. Terry said, "It won't hurt if he sleeps with us, will it?"
>
> "No," I replied, "It won't hurt this one time." Terry hoisted Mumbles onto the bed, and we were both nearly drowned with kisses. I was amused by all of this and not too concerned, as Mumbles usually sleeps at the bottom of the bed and gets off after 30 minutes or so. Not last night. He set his back nearer and nearer to the middle of the bed. I didn't get any sleep, with him on one side and Terry on the other complaining about Mumbles's heavy breathing. He's going on Terry's side next time. The question is, how long was he plotting this action?

If at all possible, Bassets really should have a bed of their own—on the floor. Here's the reason: As Bassets age, they tend to have a lot of problems with jumping up—and **down.** They are not built for it! Even young dogs can slip a disk, something you do not want happening. If your Basset is used to sleeping with you on your bed, there may come a time when he won't be able to, either for his health reasons or yours. Then you're in trouble, and both of you are in for long, sleepless nights. There he lies, moaning and groaning and sticking his miserable wet snout in your face while you're trying to sleep. Avoid the problem by getting him used to sleeping peacefully in his own bed! On a more positive note: The bed can and should be in your room with you. Dogs do not like to sleep in rooms alone. They want to be with you, and you should consider it a compliment. Besides, it's cozier that way.

"What's a six-letter word for hungry? First letter is 'h,' second letter is 'u.'"

I must confess, however, that it's easier to talk about having Bassets sleep in their own beds than actually having them do so. A case in point from Maureen Mericle:

I got Murphy when I was in graduate school. I was the typical poor student and slept in a one-room efficiency on a mattress. Murphy had a nice bed of her own, but preferred to sleep on my futon, which I didn't allow. Yet every morning when I woke up, Murphy was on my bed. I realized that she was waiting deliberately until I fell asleep (and I'm a light sleeper) and then creeping stealthily into my bed. One night I had two out-of-town girlfriends sleeping over, and all of us were sleeping on that little futon. Sure enough, the next morning, all three of us were barely on the mattress, extremities hanging off, and there was Murphy, a little queen, right in the middle. None of us had woken up.

Judith Schmidt tells a lovely tale about her late Chelsea, a dog we on Basset-L had all grown to love:

For the last five years of Chelsea's charmed and charming life, I helped her into the double guest bed each night. I made and changed it as if it

Chelsea and friend asleep in her bed. (Judith Schmidt)

were ours, and I tried to brace any overnight guests for the inevitable sad Basset-pouting that they would surely incur if they refused to let Chelsea sleep in her own bed. Our friends and family thought a full-sized human bed for a dog was a bit eccentric—especially since we had to lift her butt into bed for her!

Dotti Elliott remarks that sleeping with a Basset Hound is a lot like sleeping with a watermelon—a hot, hairy watermelon, somewhat overripe.

Rusty Hesskamp being eaten by his Bassets, out of bed!

Rusty Hesskamp writes:

I share my little full-sized bed with six hounds. I don't know where I'd put a wife if I had one. Perhaps with a pillow on the floor—that's probably all my pack would allow.

Susan Spiegle writes: "Cookie can suck the drapes into her mouth when she snores and blow them out when she exhales." Now that's a bedtime trick.

Writes Erma Ross:

Our late, sweet, beloved Rosie had a mean streak when she was jostled while sleeping. She would climb into the middle of the bed to doze, positioning herself so that when it was time for us to get into bed, she had to be moved. When that happened, she'd growl to the point of snapping at us. Since we got her from the shelter and didn't know her previous life, we figured someone may have done something to her at those times which caused this reaction.

I wouldn't be too sure about this. Our precious Mugwump, who has been ours since early puppyhood, does the same thing. The generally perfect temper of the Basset sometimes dissolves in the face of food or sleep disturbance. They are very serious about these things! I once woke Ruby up out of a sound sleep and she leapt straight up into the air and bit my face. A

Scully needs a little reassurance at night before he goes to bed. (KT Flusser)

tetanus shot and a round of antibiotics later, I know the somber truth of the old adage: "Let sleeping dogs lie." Well, what if your Basset won't go to sleep at night? KT Flusser has trouble with her Scully in this regard and has solved the problem in a somewhat unusual way. In fact, the nightly ritual works this way:

> In order for Scully to be okay with going into his crate at night, we HAVE TO sing him a song that pretty much goes like this: "I know a little boy who has to go to bed. . . . " (Repeat lyric about 20 times.)

It's to be remembered that Bassets are extremely vocal dogs themselves and enjoy being spoken to.

Gretchen Laffert says that Zach sleeps very well in his own bed at night. But:

> When he awakes early in the morning (around 4 A.M.), he starts to cry. This cry is designated for me: "Mom, I want to come sleep with you and Dad." If we let him continue to cry, he wakes up the other two dogs, and then we all have to get up. I have learned that it is best to get up and help Zach into our bed. . . . The bad thing is that Zach functions as a

sleeping pill. Usually I will put my arm around him and we cuddle. Oh, how nice and comfortable it is to snuggle with Zach. I am then lulled back to sleep by his snoring and . . . boing! We have overslept again!

David Derf uses typical Basset owner care in this regard:

I will gently pet Max until I see his eyes move, then I'll tell him, "Max, I'm gonna move you, I'm gonna move you." Then I pick him up (all two tons of him) and lay him at the foot of the bed.

One solution is to simply give in. Writes JoAnne Smith:

My daughter and her husband slept in a queen-sized waterbed until they acquired Earl and Augustus turned into the world's largest Basset (97 pounds, and none of it fat). With four Bassets, and one of them the size of two, they solved the problem by purchasing a king-sized waterbed and placing it next to the queen. Luckily they have a big bedroom.

Sometimes Bassets walk in their sleep. Judith Schmidt writes:

Our late Chelsea used to sleepwalk! Usually she just moved—very slowly—from one spot mid-living room floor to a spot behind the desk or between chairs. She never raised her eyes or responded to my speech. One Christmas we put the tree in her sleeping cubby. Chelsea would rise slowly to her feet and start for her usual spot, now filled with tree and packages. BUMP! Prickles in the nose! Reproachful, disgusted look shot at humans in the room.

Patty Nordstrom's beautiful Smuckers has, unfortunately, a rather unpleasant bedtime trick:

Does anyone have problems with a bed-wetting Basset? When we have guests, Karl, Smuckers, and I sleep on the sleeper sofa and the guests sleep in our bed. After they leave and the sheets have been changed, Smuckers feels it is her duty to urinate on the bed. I always keep a plastic sheet on the mattress to save the bed. What is she trying to accomplish, except to make me really angry?

Gretchen Laffert had one answer:

> *Maybe she smells the company's odor even after you change the sheets.*
> *Try using some sort of spray or powder that you use when "the family"*
> *sleeps in the bed. After guests have used the bed and the linens are*
> *changed, sprinkle or spray "the family scent" on the bed.*

Dennis Owen simply remarks:

> *I've had many Bassets over the last 30 years, and not one had the same*
> *personality. Charlie Dog slept upside down and slid off the chair or sofa*
> *at least once daily.*

I've heard it claimed by people, who should know better, that Bassets (indeed all dogs) prefer to sleep with their heads to the north, thus to be in sync with the earth's magnetic poles. I have nothing much to add to this remark except to say that it is not true. A Basset will sleep in any and all directions at once.

In short (or long), there are as many Basset sleeping styles as there are sleeping Bassets. Sweet dreams to all of them.

Are Bassets any better in the morning?

Bassets not only have bedtime tricks, but waking-up tricks, too. Sue Lockhart reports that her Basset, Louise, "once woke up from a nap and stretched out on her side for a big yawn. Her ear fell into her wide open mouth and, naturally, when she closed her mouth she bit her ear. You'd hope she'd have been embarrassed, but instead she jumped up growling and looking for whoever bit her."

Steven Kubik remarks:

> I'd like to introduce you all to the latest in alarm clock technology. This new alarm clock is self-running, needs no electricity, requires no winding, and has no snooze button. You can't even set the time. Yet this alarm clock will get you up at the same time every day—6:30 A.M. (whether you want to get up or not). It is not available in stores or advertised on TV. Her name is Lorelei, and she's a Basset Hound Alarm Clock. She will jump on the bed and stand on my chest whining (or growling) in various octaves and volumes until I get up. If anyone knows how to disable this alarm, please contact me, as I need some sleep.

Perhaps, as Debbie Hatt suggests, Steve should get the deluxe model. Hers, apparently, has this additional feature:

> If you try to pull the covers over your head and go back to sleep, the deluxe Basset Alarm jumps on the bed and **digs you out.** The only way to disable the Basset Alarm is to get up and feed it.

Noah Stewart's 65-pound Buster, another Basset Alarm, has his timer set for 5:15. He stands on Noah's chest and washes his face "until I get up and head downstairs to make coffee. Then *he* gets into my bed and stays there until 6:15, because he's learned that I don't take him out for at least an hour after I get up."

Amy Zeremski's Basset, Raleigh, uses various waking-up tactics, depending on who is the object:

> For my husband, all that is required is some intense staring, perhaps accompanied by a noisy Basset yawn, headshake, and flopping jowls. If that doesn't work, then a single paw on the bed is guaranteed to be

enough. For me, he starts with a soft whine and both paws on the bed to try to get a cold wet nose in the general vicinity of my face. If I manage to roll out of reach, then he walks over to the trash can and starts barking. As a last resort he will walk out of the room and make dangerous soft rustling noises, which almost certainly means he's getting into trouble eating my thesis or shoes or. . . .

My four Bassets have four distinctly different styles of requesting entrance to my bedroom, so they can get me up. Only three of them work. Freddie does the conventional high-pitched, desperate whine, which gets higher-pitched and more desperate as the seconds pass. Ruby begins a frantic snorting and sighing and groaning. Mugwump just slams her fat body against the door over and over. Miles sits silently outside the door, waiting patiently for someone to open it. No one does.

What is "butt-bonding"?

Butt-bonding, a term coined by Jerry Evenden, is a habit whereby the sleeping Basset, more often than not, slings his rear end in your face during the night, often with less than pleasant consequences for the human recipient of this rather peculiar behavior.

Jennifer Beezley writes:

> My husband has been out of town. At night, our Basset, Lucy, sleeps on my husband's pillow, facing the door, protecting me. I appreciate the sentiment, but I wake up in the morning with Basset Butt in my face. I know we're family, but come on, some things are private.

Like all of our canine friends, Basset Hounds do not have the sense of propriety that we humans would like them to display. They greet other dogs by thrusting their noses under the other dogs' tails, urinate to leave a message, and mount their canine friends to show they are superior to them. None of this, of course, thrills us, but remember it is natural behavior. As far as I can tell, however, butt-bonding is unique to the Basset species. I think it means, "I am very comfortable here, but you could move over just a little more."

Our Ruby is a double danger in bed. She likes to butt-bond, but her intestinal gas control isn't all one might hope for. In fact, the bedroom resembles a particularly fetid evening in the Dismal Swamp. If you switch her around, however, she tends to forget who or what she really is, and if wakened, becomes a Rottweiler, attacking whatever face happens to be nearest her own. I'd like to say I have solved the problem by bravely banishing Ruby from the bedroom. But then she howls. I've settled for Swamp Thing.

How many ways can a Basset wag its tail?

Plenty, apparently. There is, for example, the Basset's "full circle wag"—slowly round and round. This means your dog has spotted a rabbit in the bushes.

There is Watson's "rattlesnake wag," which shows up when Anita Wright asks, "Where's my precious baby?" (Watson has a white-tipped tail, which gives him away, just like a snake in the grass.)

Bassets also thump their tails hard and slowly on the kitchen floor, meaning, "Feed me, please."

A weak partial wag indicates uncertainty.

A tail at "half-staff" means, "Watch out, I am highly annoyed."

Can Basset hair be spun into a coat?

Of course not. Why would anyone ever think that it could? Even the redoubtable Kenall Crolius and Anne Montgomery, in their timeless work, *Knitting With Dog Hair*, confess themselves stumped at this challenge. They do suggest that you scatter your recyclable Basset hair onto the fibers of "more spinnable" dog hair and work from that. Well, to each his own. The cover of the book does feature a lovely Basset wearing an extremely chic hat that looks like it is made out of an Old English Sheep Dog. Very nice indeed.

Can Bassets be aggressive?

Not usually, but when their dander is up, they are capable of landing a good (or bad) bite. See "Do Bassets Have Any Special Bedtime Tricks?" above.

Karl Heege says that his Basset, Watson, is very aggressive at his supper dish. He attacks it without mercy. Karl's female Basset is braver, however. She goes after the concrete deer in the neighbor's yard.

A strange thing in this regard happened to Steve Kirkpatrick with his Basset, Basil. He writes:

> Basil the Basset is normally a very easygoing hound. But a few weeks ago, Basil went into the backyard and didn't come back right away. So I went looking for him. I found him on the side of the house rummaging through the trash can. (We have a can with latching handles, but he quickly defeated that mechanism with his advanced canine intelligence.) Basil saw me coming; when I was within five feet of the can, he started barking at ME, like a dog possessed! It was as if he had turned into an attack dog. I immediately picked up a spare trash can lid to fend off his fanged advance. Then I grabbed the other trash can lid and promptly secured it on the can he had been searching through—it contained assorted chicken pieces from the previous night's dinner. I shooed Basil away from the trash area and back into the house. Once in the house he totally forgot the incident and went back to being his sweet and lovable self. What a difference 60 seconds make.

Our dog, Miles, is fiercely aggressive. He barked at a flower pot for about two hours. Two months later, he and one of our other Bassets, Flash, barked at a rocking horse all afternoon. Miles once saw a real horse, by the way. He slunk into a corner and pretended not to notice it.

Judith Schmidt's young Shelby recently had her first Halloween—and Halloween scare.

> In our neighborhood, there are plenty of older homes with big porches—and lots of lawn lamps on posts. With the nice weather, out came the lawn scarecrows! You know, the pumpkin-headed dudes lounging around the houses and lamps with scary attitudes. Shelby wasn't bothered by the

mean faces or the plastic weapons; however, she did notice that these characters did not come to visit her! She poses, wiggles, and still gets ignored. Something is terribly wrong with these new neighbors. (I have to admit, the creative neighbor who planted half a scarecrow man climbing out of a fake grave really confounded Shelby!)

Many Bassets believe that discretion is indeed the better part of valor. Maureen Mericle writes:

Murphy picks all kinds of things to be terrified by. The broom is horrible, and the vacuum cleaner is truly from hell. The weirdest of all is that she is terrified, beyond all comprehension, of my **purse.**

Obviously, a woman's purse is nothing to fool around with.

On a more serious note, there have been a few recorded cases of psychotic Bassets biting out of aggression or fear. This kind of aggression usually shows up very early, and in almost no circumstance can it be altered. I am not talking about a snarl when other pets come close to his food dish. I am talking about an uninhibited bite response that can leave a serious wound. This kind of rage is the result, usually, of irresponsible breeding practices and is a genetic defect. In some cases, brain tumors have been found. You should contact the breeder and discuss your dog's behavior. A responsible breeder should be extremely alarmed and offer to take back the dog.

It is a reasonable first step to try obedience training, but you are facing a difficult path. Sadly, these dogs must often be euthanized, as treatment is risky at best. More than 4.5 million Americans are bitten by dogs every year, 800,000 of them seriously enough to require medical treatment. Fifteen people per year, usually children, are killed by dogs. (So far, none of them have been killed by Bassets.)

Do not "give away" your dog in the hopes that his problems will go away. They won't, and you may be legally liable for any injuries he may cause. Insurance companies pay out a billion dollars a year in dog-bite claims.

How good is a Basset's hearing?

Sophie (Jan Green)

Very good—when he wants it to be. In other words, it is a typical example of selective hearing, a trait also evident in recalcitrant children. From Anita Wright:

> The other night, Mumbles was lying on the settee—apparently in a coma. I said quietly to Terry, "Open the muffin pack." The TV was on, quite loud, and Terry was being careful not to make noise. I watched Mumbles come out of the coma, sit up, jump off the settee, and get onto the arm of Terry's chair.

Gretchen Laffert writes:

> When my three dogs are in the backyard, they come when I call them into the house. When they are out in the front yard, where all the street action is, they are DEAF. Zach will usually come if I say, "Zach, want something?" Annabel ignores me until I count to three. On three, I say, "Did you hear what I said?" She will then turn to look back at me and turn her head as if to say, "So?" But when she hears me walking irritably towards her, she's up like a flash, running to the house. Miss Xanadu comes every time—no fuss—as if to say, "I'm comin', Mom! I love you!"

Do Bassets get along with other pets?

You be the judge. Gretchen Laffert writes about her Basset, Annabel, and Eddie the lop-eared rabbit:

> *Everything was fine until Eddie (a male) began to experience "Love in the Spring." At that romantic season, Eddie would begin to chase the Bassets. He would catch them or sneak up on them while they were sleeping and bite them on the back, then start his "manly activity." [See "Do Bassets Enjoy Sex?" page 76.] At the end of the season, he had no use for them whatever, but as Annabel grew larger, she began to drag Eddie around the living room by his ears. In the wild, female rabbits can be very abusive to the male, and since, with her long floppy ears, Annabel probably looked like a big female rabbit to Eddie, he put up with it.*

In spite of this treatment and his sexual delusions, Gretchen reports that the unfortunate Eddie lived to be nine years old.

Bassets love company. They like you best (usually), but in your absence, they will gladly settle for other pets. Bassets come naturally in pairs (a brace, in dog parlance), and there is no better substitute for your company than the company of another Basset. In general, Bassets get along best with a dog of the opposite sex, but there's no hard and fast rule about this. I do recommend having company for your Basset, however. It may preserve the carpet, furniture, electric appliances, and your sanity. (I cannot deny that once in a blue moon or so, the pair of Bassets will think up worse things to do than either could conjure on his own, but it's a risk you must take.) Besides, it's always fun to hook a couple of them up together and walk down the street. Everyone will talk to you.

Annette Green writes:

> *Monte and I recently brought a cat into our lives. They met at the vet's office while Monte was having his annual physical. Someone found the cat on their doorstep one morning; he couldn't walk because he had been shot with buckshot. He had been at the vet's office for three weeks. When Monte and Kramer Lestat (the cat) met, they touched noses and began sniffing at various places in the examining room. I knew Kramer was the cat for us; he had a flair for following his nose, so the "boys"*

Sabrina Nicholls's Calhoune is very attached to his feline playmate.

already had a lot in common. Monte was delighted to have him live with us, and they are the best of friends. . . . They are inseparable now. When Monte, after an accident, had his leg wrapped so that only his toes were exposed, Kramer would kiss his toes.

On a slightly different note, Amy Zeremski tells of an experience her Basset, Raleigh, had with a cow in a field. At first the cows were not visible (though they had left plenty of evidence around of their presence). She remarks:

*Raleigh, who had never seen a cow before, was working overtime sniffing all the interesting smells. As we walked along, the cows suddenly appeared a hundred yards or so away. Raleigh's tail started wagging and he began walking towards the cows. The cows were also walking towards us, and Raleigh noticed that they were becoming **much** bigger. His tail wagging began to grow more hesitant, slowing down and finally stopping. For a while, Raleigh just stood there staring at the cows, who continued to amble in our general direction. Finally, he decided that caution was the better part of valor. He gave a big "WOOF," then turned around and started trotting quickly back the way we came. The cows kept* *coming, also moving more quickly. Raleigh became even more nervous. He kept looking over his shoulder, as if to say to us, "Come on, guys! I'll bark at them, but I don't know how much longer I can hold them off!" The cows seemed to think that Raleigh was calling to them ("Our master calls—we must go to him"), but since we weren't exactly sure what the cows planned on doing if they caught up with him, we decided Raleigh's strategy wasn't such a bad one and followed him out of the pasture. The cows seemed a little disappointed to see their little playmate go.*

Sometimes Bassets aren't sure what are pets and what aren't. Judith Schmidt writes:

Chelsea was about a year old on a warm prairie spring day in northeastern Colorado. It was 70 degrees in the high country sun—even though the soil was still frozen solid. Chelsea came into the kitchen through the open patio door and dropped a clod of dirt—about the size of a softball— at my feet. I said, "Yuck!" and tossed the dirt, overhand, across the backyard. Three minutes later, Chelsea was back in the house with her clod. This time I took the ball and put it in the sink. "That'll teach her to play fetch with me," I thought, and went on with my cooking. The next time I passed the sink I noticed that the clod of dirt was watching me with one watery amphibious eye! Chelsea had smelled, and unearthed, a BIG hibernating toad! I grabbed the poor guy and carried him around front, where he'd be safe from the puppy, and stuffed him under the edge of the porch.

The toad, eventually named Mongo, appeared several times over the next two years we lived in Colorado. Chelsea loved to herd him around with her nose, but he tasted too bad, apparently, for her ever to pick up again.

Toads exude an irritant that is unpleasant and sometimes poisonous to dogs. Most dogs will leave toads alone after a single encounter.

Bassets and birds are a story unto themselves. Once we had two parakeets, a yellow one and a blue one. They both seemed to think it was the funniest thing in the world to fly around and dive bomb the Bassets, playing them for fools, as it were. Stories like this always have an "Until one

Chelsea loved to herd Mongo the toad around with her nose.

day . . . " sequel. Sure enough, one day, as I was sitting at my computer working, I happened to notice a pale yellow feather drifting to my feet. "What the %$#@&*?" I mumbled, getting up. As I raced into the bird room, all I spied was a particularly fat Mugwump staring up at the window and one terrified and jabbering blue parakeet huddled on the curtain rod. The yellow bird was never seen again. The blue parakeet adopted a more prudent way of life.

A different sort of experience is recorded by Rodica Stoicoiu. Her late beloved Blue Front Amazon parrot, Augustine, was not one to be pushed around by a couple of Basset Hounds:

> Augustine long had the run of the house. I had even taught her to come on command and, like a good parrot, she not only followed the command (obviously she was not related to Bassets), but she repeated the command as well, muttering, "Come here, come here," as she waddled across the floor to me. [Waddling is a trait parrots do have in common with Bassets, I notice.] When she was five years old, we brought home two Basset puppies and proceeded to obedience train our new hounds. Strangely enough, this seemed to work. One day, while standing on the coffee table, Augustine called, "Come here, come here," as usual, but instead of me, she got two large Basset noses in her face. So she nailed them right between the nostrils. I think she enjoyed the resultant howls (she also liked crying babies and opera) and began to call the dogs to her cage on a regular basis. Without fail, they would show up, stick their noses in her cage, and then run for their lives when she bit them. It took a couple of weeks to decide that maybe this wasn't such a good idea after all. To this day I feel sure that one of the reasons my Bassets won't come on command is because of Augustine's aversion dog training technique. [Well, that may be. On the other hand, they probably won't come simply because they're Bassets. If one is a Basset, I guess, it's enough simply to be. One shouldn't have to do things, too.]

A hard-to-top tale is offered by Marisabel Boyd about her three-month-old Basset, Chivas:

> The geese at our beach house had been laying eggs in their nest for several weekends, and Chivas had been sniffing warily at them. Finally

he decided to get a bit closer; the geese went berserk, hissing at him and flapping their wings frantically. A couple of hours later, our gardener hosed down the geese inside their picket fence area. The nest was outside, and Chivas went over to investigate it. He sniffed the eggs with great curiosity and suddenly lay down gently on them (this was strange as he usually flops down) and started Ahrooooooooing, which he had never done before. An hour later the geese were let out and came flying at him in a rage. He ran like a bolt towards the house, then turned around and started barking at the geese. He then started to dig a hole. Throughout the afternoon the hole got bigger and he started piling all kinds of things inside, including a shoe, a mop, his favorite toy, and some sticks. Later, when we were packing up to leave, he went to his nest and flopped down and Ahroooooooed, while looking at the geese with a superior look that seemed to say, "Hey you feathered weirdos, my nest is bigger and better than yours."

Do Bassets enjoy sex?

Yes, but they don't seem to be very good at it. (See "Do Bassets Get Along with Other Pets?" page 71.) Most of my reading on the subject seems to indicate they need a little advice and coaching in this regard because of their ungainly anatomy. I wonder about this. Crocodiles and tortoises seem to manage all right, and they're not exactly swanlike. Speaking of swans, I've always wondered how . . . well, never mind, let's get on to the next topic. But first, another answer to this question: Not if they have to get off the couch to participate.

Do Bassets make good watch dogs?

GRACIE   Pam Posey-Tanzey

Absolutely. They frequently drool thieves to death. Jennifer Jamieson says that Bassets make excellent watch dogs. They watch for sausage. In the same vein, Anita Wright says:

> Watson is an excellent watch dog. If we are having a TV dinner, he will sit and watch the food for hours, until it is cleared away.

Amanda Sherwin says:

> Bassets are fine watch dogs. You can tell the time by them. Especially meal time.

Sue Lockhart writes:

> While I was living in an apartment with Louise, my long-gone first Basset, the dishwasher broke. I had asked the manger to let me know when it was going to be repaired so I could confine the dog, but he forgot. I came home to find a note saying the dishwasher couldn't be repaired because of the dog. Concerned about a possible nasty streak of Louise's that I hadn't seen, I asked the manager what had happened. It seems that when this total stranger entered the apartment, Louise was so glad to see him that when he sat down to repair the dishwasher, she crawled in his lap to snuggle and wouldn't get up.

Bassets have been known to stand by calmly watching thieves dismantle the family car. They will leave this occupation only to bark viciously at a friendly neighbor walking down the street with a stroller.

Our dog, Flash, never barked when we had company; he stood mute in the face of letter carriers, neighbors, and magazine salespeople. He did, however, go into a bark-frenzy whenever we **left** the house, thus alerting the entire immediate world that we had left home and the house was now available for ransacking.

Even if Bassets don't make such hot watch dogs, however, they apparently make tempting prey. Coleen McKinnell and her family were vacationing at Sproat Lake on Vancouver Island in Canada. Her son, Fraser, had their Basset, Bailey, at his heels when a friend saw a **cougar** charging them from the woods!

> He screamed, "Cougar!" at which point I came running out of the cabin to the deck just in time to see the cougar leap on Bailey and roll her over. My son reacted quickly and, turning around, kicked the cougar in the face. The cougar released the Basset and started to run into the bushes. Bailey started to chase it, and my son started to chase her! I was screaming helplessly from the deck and then saw—about 20 yards away—a second cougar sitting calmly on a rock and watching the whole proceeding. Somehow Fraser managed to scoop up the dog and get into the cabin with the rest of the kids.

Lucky Bailey to have such a smart and courageous friend as Fraser. Later the two cougars were caught and had to be shot because of their utter fearlessness of human beings.

Connie Frey's Suzie-Q is not going to be caught in such a situation:

> We have a couple of crows in our backyard; every time she hears them, she comes flying with her ears trailing behind her and hides by our feet. We are trying to housebreak her, and it's kind of hard explaining that this is where she needs to go, when there are all these foreign creatures around. Recently she was looking out the back window when a blue jay flew up to the bird feeder. Suzie-Q ran and hid behind the couch. So much for the watch dog!

Karen Clemente's Basset, Ashley, is not so much a watch dog, either. But she makes a remarkable baby-sitter. Once, when Karen had to step out of the baby's room for a tissue:

> Ashley immediately lay in front of the baby so that Jason could not leave the room. When he tried at first, she knocked him gently down on his butt so he wouldn't go out. When that expedient proved only temporary, she pulled him back by grabbing the back of his shirt. I was sooooo proud of her!

Are Bassets helpful during emergencies?

Actually, Bassets are much more likely to create emergencies rather than solve them. Even when not the actual cause of the emergency, they are likely to complicate an already bad situation. During Hurricane Fran, Sue Lockhart was trapped at home with Sophie and Boss. Her driveway was blocked by a downed tree entangled with power lines, and her roof was leaking, too. Still, she writes, "I would have gotten off easily were it not for the Bassets. Currently I am not speaking to either of them." Sue had done quite a lot of work over the previous few years waterproofing her basement, but all was for naught. The Bassets had dug themselves a cozy hole right next to the foundation, which allowed a torrent of water to penetrate the basement and attack her heater, washer, and dryer. Sue is not at all certain that her homeowner's insurance covers "acts of dogs."

Do Bassets have ESP?

You bet. They can predict thunderstorms, dinnertime, and always know when you're planning a trip, with or without them. They seem to know other things, too. Amy Zeremski writes:

> I was walking Augie and Raleigh one day and was talking to a man we had met a couple of times before in the neighborhood. He and his two children had gotten out of their minivan to pet the Bassets. (Augie and Raleigh really soak up things like this.) His wife, who is blind, stayed in the back of the minivan, but the door was open. The man asked his wife if she wanted to say hello to the dogs, and she said yes. I took the dogs over to the van, a little worried that they might just jump in and startle the woman. (They generally see any open car door as an invitation to get in and go for a ride.) To my surprise, they went one at a time, each putting only the front paws into the car, and presented their heads to be petted. It seemed as if they sensed somehow that she couldn't see them and that they should take it easy and just say, "Hello."

"I see an unexpected trip in your future."

Are Bassets Democrats or Republicans?

Most Bassets are registered Democrats, but they frequently cross party lines and vote Republican. By nature, of course, Bassets are independent (unlike Beagles who always vote Democratic and Afghans who vote the straight GOP ticket), but they are wise enough to know that in many states one needs to have a party affiliation to vote in the primaries. Bassets tend to be liberal on social issues and particularly active in the animal rights movement, but they are fiscally conservative and stand up (sort of) for a strong national defense.

Amanda Sherwin agrees that Bassets are independents; they'll sell their votes for the best belly rub. "By the way," she writes, "they'll never make it to the White House. They would be stopped by BellyGates."

Jennifer Beezley's Lucy is a strong Democrat. As she states, "She doesn't think Dole is a 'dog' man." Jennifer's husband was appalled when Jennifer told the world that his dog was a Democrat, but says Jennifer, "that's just the way it is."

Patty Nordstrom thinks Smuckers would make a great politician herself. "She loves to give speeches and press the flesh (especially if the flesh is rubbing her belly). She would be overjoyed to attend political dinners— even if the food was bad, as long as it was people food. I don't think she cares about what party she belongs to." Let's face it, Bassets enjoy any kind of party, especially if cake and ice cream are served.

Anne Whitacre writes: "One time I took Spencer to a political fund-raiser, and right at the 'important' moment in the candidate's speech, a loud snore came from the floor; yep, it was Spencer." Bassets know what's important in life.

Are Bassets religious?

Sometimes. In my Basset family, Miles is an Episcopalian turned Baptist, Ruby a lapsed Catholic, and Mugwump an atheist. This seems to be a fairly standard assortment. Since most churches do not allow dogs, Sunday schooling at home is a good idea. It certainly wouldn't hurt anything.

Perhaps if Bassets practice religion, it is Zen Buddhism. Like the great Zen Masters of old, they are capable of sitting for extraordinarily long periods. They are also extremely centered (self-centered) and appear to be meditating on what is truly important in the world—namely themselves.

Jennifer Jamieson believes that all Bassets are religious. "They pray for food."

Barbara Couillard says that her Sophie is religious "to the extent that when she's done something wrong, the look she gives me says, 'The Devil made me do it, Mom!'"

On a more conventional note, Judith Schmidt tells me that her late Chelsea was a Presbyterian (quite a surprise to Judith, who is an Episcopalian). She writes:

> When Chelsea was five, we moved right next door to a Presbyterian church. The only service that the 12-member congregation held was at 8:45 on Sundays. Chelsea always managed to request an "out" between 8:15 and 8:30 so she could greet the churchgoers. During warm summer days she would lie in the yard and listen to the hymns and homilies wafting out the open windows, and she never howled at the bell like some of the other dogs in the neighborhood. And she was always respectful if the part-time pastor stopped to pat Chelsea and ask her if she had enjoyed the sermon. Indeed, I have gotten two condolence cards from church members since Chelsea's death in May.

Dallas-Alice, owned by Donna Matushak-Funk

What are Bassets' favorite TV shows?

Answers on the Basset List varied. The Maytag commercial seemed a natural and favorite choice, along with "Great Chefs." But Bassets are far more eclectic than that. Kathryn Walbert writes:

> Our Basset, Feynmann, actually watches rodeo with great interest, believe it or not! Dave was watching the rodeo with her one day and started flipping channels during a commercial. Feynmann looked at the TV, then at the remote, then at Dave, then back at the remote and again at Dave and voiced her displeasure with a "Wurrrr." Once he switched back to the rodeo, she settled back down and watched. The bull ride, incidentally, seemed to be her favorite part. . . . In fact, she'll watch anything with animals on it pretty intently. Once, when we were watching a PBS program on wolves, she ran up to the TV and sniffed, then ran to the window to see if they were outside.

Lisa Slinsky writes:

> The other night I was watching TV on one sofa with Mona in my lap, while Bill was on the other with Baxter. A commercial starring a Basset Hound came on, and Mona sat upright and watched the whole thing. I know I'm anthropomorphizing, but I would swear that she recognized that they were of the same kind. I have never seen her watch anything so intently before (except last year's World Series).

Anne Whitacre writes:

> I used to date someone who told me Spencer needed a "man" to "teach him about beer and nachos and stuff." I came home once to see Spencer

with a baseball cap on, eagerly snuffling nachos and watching football on television with my (then) boyfriend.

Speaking of televisions, remote controls are a blessing to the breed. As Barb Bates writes:

[My Basset, Snoopy] loves remotes. We got him in July and immediately started rescuing remotes from his jaws. The TV remote was history first, but only after several attempts. The VCR remote was next; the cable box remote has teeth marks but still works. In this lazy couch potato world, one must have a TV and VCR remote, so off to the store I went to buy a generic remote. I brought it home, along with all the other stuff you have to buy while you're at Wal-Mart, and put the sack on the floor. Snoopy nosed through it, found the remote (still in the package), and took off with it. I'm sure he thought I had bought it just for him. It was rescued and after two months is still operational, although it does have a few teeth marks in it.

Speaking of television, I noticed that our foster dog, Flash, chews his ears while watching. He seems particularly fond of the Sunday morning political chat shows and sits in the living room during the entire program, watching and chewing his ears thoughtfully. When I mentioned this to Basset-L, JoAnne Smith retorted: "When I listen to politicians, I want to chew my ears too." Apparently, ear chewing is not restricted to television. Barbara Winters writes:

My three-year-old Roadie has chewed on his ears since I brought him home as a puppy. Actually, he doesn't really chew them as much as he sucks on them. As soon as he is done eating, he flips his ear into his mouth and sucks on it while at the same time licking his bowl to make sure he has gotten every last molecule of food. Sometimes he sucks both ears, though not at the same time. My friends are so amazed that they stop by the house at Basset feeding time, just so they can watch him suck his ears. Aren't we lucky to be owned by such dogs?

This definitely seems to be a trait peculiar to Bassets.

Can Bassets be trusted with credit cards?

In general, Bassets have terrible credit. My Mugwump was out the door with her AKC Visa card five minutes after it arrived—heading, no doubt, for a gourmet food store and trying to convince the clerk that it was, in fact, her picture in the corner.

Teresa Wrenn, however, had a different experience. She has two phone lines, one unlisted and the other listed under the name of her Basset Hound, Tyler. (Don't ask me to explain this. We basseteers are a peculiar lot.) Anyway, she writes:

> What has happened is that Tyler has received NUMEROUS invitations to respond immediately for credit cards with up to $10,000 worth of credit (which is twice as much as I can get). He also gets offers for insurance policies and tax planning, and he receives loads of sample products in the mail. One company, a database vendor, decided that Tyler was the owner of the house and had his salary listed at $58,000.

Tyler has since crossed the Rainbow Bridge, but the database vendor still has the deceased Basset as the deed holder to the property. When she finally gets around to selling the house, Teresa is expecting the closing from hell. The lesson from all this should be obvious: If you must have a phone for your Basset, make sure that it has an unlisted number.

Beth Fuller adds:

> I, too, have Bassets who have mysteriously made it onto mailing lists. Daisy (age 12, who had a mastectomy two years ago) gets invitations to breast cancer screenings at a local hospital and gets coupons from the Honey Baked Ham Company! Rosebud gets free software from all the online services and chances to subscribe to book and music clubs, and she also got an application for a credit card. I'm sorry to say that she was rejected for the credit card, though. I filled out the application for her and told them that she did not have a social security number and had never held a paying job. I explained that Rosebud was a beautiful Basset who lived with me and who would not abuse her credit card. I also mentioned that Rosebud would not require a very high credit limit, as her expenses are limited to food and vet bills.

"Well, they must have raised her credit limit again."

1st ▮▮▮▮▮ BANKCARD
▮▮ DeLaVina Street
Santa Barbara, CA 93105

FINAL ATTEMPT

Dear Mr. Tyler,
We are trying to reach you.   CREDIT APPROVED FOR:
Your $5,000 credit limit <u>has been</u>
<u>Approved</u>
Call me at 1-900-▮▮-1100* <u>Now</u>

Sincerely,   Mr. M. Tyler
John ▮▮▮▮   ▮ Hylan Bl.
Card Member Services   Staten Island, NY 10305-2074

Please have this personal
<u>Reference#</u> ready when calling

        1▮22-014-▮▮

|..ıllll.....ıll.ll....l.l....l.lll...l....l.l..ll..l.l

Tyler has been approved for a $5,000 credit line.

Unfortunately, Beth never heard back from the credit card company.

To this Annette Green writes:

> I loved the story of how Daisy and Rosebud had their names on several mailing lists. I once ordered the Dr. Seuss collection of books for the children of some friends and relatives. When I placed the order, they asked for the name of the child in my household, so naturally I gave them Monte's name. Since then I have received telemarketing calls wanting to know if Monte would be interested in some nature books as well as various others. I usually get a laugh from the person on the other end of the line when they are told that Monte is a Basset Hound and, even though he has a Ph.D. (Dr. Robert Montague), he does not read.

Do Bassets Have Good Manners?

Probably not as nice as Poodles, but maybe better than your brother-in-law. Susan Hurt asks, "Why do Bassets feel obliged to stick their tongues out all the way when they yawn? Perdita's breath doesn't smell all that great, but at least I can get a good view of her teeth." Karen Clemente adds that Ashley waits until she is looking her in the face before burping. "Even if I'm in another room or upstairs when she finishes her dinner, no matter how long it takes for me to come by her, she manages to burp in my face anyway. She saves them just for me." Maybe it's a sign of true love. Certain other bodily functions, smells, and noises, although discussed enthusiastically and in detail on Basset-L, will be mercifully omitted from this text.

Training the Basset: An Exercise in Futility?

Can I housebreak my Basset?

Yes, but you may break first. The same quality that makes the Basset an untiring, persistent dog in the hunting field is called "cussed stubbornness" at other times. It's important to remember that Bassets are bred to be stubborn. Patience is the key. Because of their unusual anatomy, even the best-hearted, most willing Basset is no easy animal to housebreak. Consider the following, from Judy Trenck:

> We have a doggie door, and Angel and Big Girl were getting used to going in and out whenever they needed. One day, Angel decided it was time for her to go out, so she pulled her front end out the doggie door; then something caught her attention, so she stopped, front end outside, back end in the house. She stood there a few seconds, then squatted and peed right where she was. In her mind, since the front end was outside, she didn't need to worry about where the back end was!

It's nice to know that Angel eventually entered a show career and became a Champion. We hope her toileting skills improved as well.

Bassets, by the way, prefer to urinate on the softest and most luxurious material available. Tile floors have almost no allure for them, but expensive carpeting is irresistible. To keep your Basset from urinating in his training crate, use less absorbent materials that will make it seem less attractive to him. Never use ammonia-based products to clean up pet urine. The reason? Ammonia and urine are made up of the same ingredients and smell alike to your dog. Cleaning a urine-soaked area with ammonia is saying, "Yes, this is certainly a good spot, isn't it?" Try using bleach. It completely eliminates the odor.

Most pet owner books will tell you to clean up after your dog as soon as possible. Perhaps they are operating under the assumption that, left to their own devices, pet owners will not clean up after their pets as soon as possible. Perhaps they think that your average pet owner will say to herself, "Why, look at that! Puppy urine and messes all over the floor. Perhaps I'll clean it up later, after I've done the dishes." This book assumes that yes, indeed, you will clean up messes as soon as possible after you notice them, which doesn't usually take long.

Gretchen Laffert suggests putting the dog in his crate and making him stay there when you are not actively watching or playing with him. After a reasonable time alone, take him outside and stay with him until has done his business. Do not let him wander around the entire yard snooping freely; keep him within a restricted area, so that he knows this is not a frivolous expedition. When he does go, praise him—immensely. Go wild with joy. Believe it or not, your Basset actually does want to please you; he just isn't always sure how yet. As Gretchen says, "These Bassets are very intelligent, but you need to convince them that they are!"

A couple of caveats: Never try to push a dog's nose into his mess if he has made a mistake. It won't work, and it will confuse and possibly frighten him. (If you're under the impression that dog mess smells as bad to the dog as it does to us, however, you're mistaken. The only odors that naturally repel dogs are certain chemical ones. Vomit, feces, urine, carrion, and so forth are merely of scientific interest to the Basset.)

Never hit your dog for making a housebreaking error. Striking an animal for any reason is wrong, and it certainly is ineffectual in the housebreaking department. A Basset under four months of age is not completely

Cleo (Jeanne McBride)

in control of his sphincter muscles, for one thing, and is no more responsible than a two-year-old human being, who also sometimes makes similar mistakes. Your puppy will need to eliminate **something** at least eight times a day. The younger the puppy, the more often he will need to "go." Take your dog out the same door to the same place every time. Routine helps him get the idea. Again, praise him lavishly. Your Basset adores being praised, even if, at first, he is not quite certain as to the reason of the sudden adulation. Being rather single-minded, he may confuse the issue, thinking that the praise is due to his having functioned at all, rather than for functioning in the correct place. It will take time. Maybe a lot of time. Be calm. By the time your Basset gets to high school, he will be housetrained!

It may be a good idea to reduce water intake in the evening. Sometimes dogs drink more than they need, just for something to do. Do **not** withhold water from your pet if he seems really thirsty, though. Some trainers recommend giving your dog ice cubes instead of water in the evening. The problem with this suggestion is twofold: First, many dogs don't like ice cubes, and second, ice cubes are not thirst quenching. In fact, they dehydrate. The coolness of the melting cube may taste fine, but in fact it takes more energy to dissolve the cube than the dog (or you) gets from it. That's why you can't eat snow when you're thirsty—same principle. For water to act in its natural function, it must be in liquid form.

When we were Basset-sitting for our friend, Shellie Smith, we noticed that her Basset, Fern, was TOO well housebroken, if you can imagine such a thing. Shellie doesn't have a fenced yard, so she takes Fern out for several walks a day (more than she got around here, believe me). When I let Fern out to accomplish her mission after meals, she refused to do so until I put her on a leash. Then she went immediately, but not otherwise. If no leash was forthcoming, she'd wander blankly around the yard for 15 minutes, come back in the house, and whine until the leash came out.

What is the best kind of collar to use?

Keep a buckle or quick-snap collar on your dog at all times. This collar should carry his identification tags, dog license, and rabies tag. For training purposes, you may wish to use a training collar (choke or slip chain), self-correcting collar, or halter. Unless you know how to use these devices safely and effectively, take an obedience class with your Basset. You'll learn more than he will, but that's the point. He'll enjoy himself immensely, watching you learn how to "handle" him, and you'll pick up some useful tips about dog training.

Slip or choke collars should always be removed when not in use; otherwise, you're asking for your Basset to strangle himself.

Many Basset owners like harnesses for their dogs. Harnesses have the advantage of not putting pressure on your dog's neck, and the no-pull kind are useful for controlling your dog. I should warn you, though, that harnesses do nothing to help train your dog or stop the pulling problem. If you use one because your Basset pulls (and they are terrific pullers—their low center of gravity makes them immensely strong), you're not solving the problem by using a harness; you're only treating the symptoms.

As for leashes, the latest advance is the Flexi leash, which combines freedom and control. Some kinds provide 32 feet of "leeway," although 16 feet is more standard. Flexi leashes give your dog a sense of freedom and you a sense of control. What more could one ask for?

How do I choose a good obedience class?

GRACIE   Pam Posey-Tanzey

Obedience classes are for you as much as for your Basset. You need to take classes together. Some classes are on a one-to-one basis, while others are geared for groups. The advantage of group training is that it helps socialize your dog, as well as helps him deal with distractions. The best groups are divided by age and ability of dogs and should have no more than eight class members.

When seeking out an obedience class, get references from Basset-owned friends or talk to your local kennel club. Not every dog trainer is used to working with hounds. Most have gotten their experience with Labradors or Golden Retrievers, dogs whose personalities are perfect for obedience classes. Bassets, who can most benefit from such classes, are more of a challenge for them. Some trainers frankly will not work with hounds. They know when they've been beaten.

Even if the prospective trainer declares herself willing to take on a Basset Hound, inquire as to whether she believes in rewarding dogs with treats. If she says "No," think about going to another trainer. Bassets respond to food training very well. You will not "spoil" your dog by treating him. You're simply using the most effective way to get the best response from a Basset Hound.

It's not enough to go to class once a week, however. You must do your homework and work with your hound every day. Otherwise, valuable lessons learned at school may be soon forgotten—by both of you. Practice, practice, practice.

Well, what does a Basset need to know, anyway?

Luckily, Bassets already know all the basic skills. They can sit, lie down, come, and stay. They can even heel. The trick, of course, is having the dog demonstrate these high-level abilities when you ask him to.

In training a dog, the first thing you need to do is to get his attention. With most dogs, this is pretty easy. You know you have their attention because they'll prick up their ears. Bassets never prick up their ears, but they will sometimes actually look in your direction. You'll have to be content with that.

There are many, many good books on the market about dog training. Just remember, everything requires more patience with a Basset than with other breeds.

Never take the advice of a dog trainer who recommends harsh methods or who disdains using food as an incentive. Bassets are delicate creatures, and can be crushed by a rough word. Worse yet, they might even ignore you. But all Bassets respond remarkably well to food. Keep your expectations within reason, and your oh-so-reasonable (and greedy) Basset Hound will meet you halfway, as long as he doesn't have to get off the couch.

Never lose your temper, but never lose hope either. You can indeed learn to get your Basset to acquiesce, at least most of the time, to your desires. You will never have a dog-slave, but then, you never wanted one, did you?

Do Bassets respond to discipline?

In a weird way. JoAnne Smith says:

> When Basset's don't want to move, they increase their weight by about a ton and suction cup their big feet to the ground. They do, however, respond to bribes. All our dogs will answer to, "Who wants to come in/ go out for a cookie?" They will wake from a sound sleep at the word "cookie." Some of the time they will move if I say, "March! Hup-two-free-fo!" Earl will come, wagging his tail, if I show him a rolled-up newspaper and say, "Earl! Do you want me to get my wacker?" Now bear in mind Earl has never been whacked, but he must want to because he comes so cheerfully when I threaten to whack him. He just wiggles and wags as if he's saying, "Oh, goodie! I'm gonna get whacked." One look at this performance and you couldn't whack him if you wanted to. It's too funny.

JoAnne Smith's Earl keeps everyone entertained, even out of the clown costume.

Bassets are very, very sensitive creatures and simply do not respond well to threats or to being struck. Never ever hit your Basset Hound. A firm glare (while trying not to smile) works best, along with a strong, "No, no, **bad, bad** dog." This may work. Then again, it may not. Assuredly, however, harsh methods of discipline not only do not work, but can destroy a relationship of love and trust. Physical restraint is sometimes necessary; physical punishment never is.

Sometimes a creative approach is called for. Moses, a Basset owned by Leslie Druschel, writes:

> Dear Long-Eared Friends, I am a very disgusted dog! For the last year and a half, I have been able to jump up to any table or counter and help myself to whatever edibles I have found waiting for me. But all that has changed. Last night my mom brought home this hateful device called a Snappy Trainer. This confounded contraption looks like a mousetrap with a plastic paddle attached to it. Now when I try to get after those tasty treats, I trigger the Snappy Trainer and it makes a loud SNAP! that makes me jump. It doesn't actually hurt me, I guess, but I don't like it. Just now I heard Mom say she's going to get another and keep it by the trash can. Not that! If any other Bassets out there read this, delete this message before your folks see it or they might buy one, too. (It wasn't expensive.) Just a warning. . . Moses.

Sometimes you will hear people recommend shaking cans full of pennies at wayward dogs, or scattering mousetraps on furniture. This may work fine with ordinary dogs, but most Bassets simply ignore such devices, after an initial exposure. Besides, it's embarrassing to have mousetraps all over the furniture. What will your guests think?

What does it mean when my Basset stares at me?

Dog-staring is not the same thing as people-staring, at least not usually. When you feel your Basset's eyes fastened upon you, it means: (a) he wants you to give him something, most likely a sandwich, but possibly a good belly rub, (b) he wants to go out for a walk, or (c) he's gone mad and is thinking about killing you. This is because, in the animal world, a strong eyeball to eyeball stare is a sign of aggression. Even in our world, a long stare is invariably regarded as an aggressive act, except between close friends or lovers. In that case, it means, "I trust you completely. Look into my eyes all you like." When dogs are staring at each other, however, it means trouble and no joke.

Now we have domesticated our canine friends to the point where they understand that our looking at them does not necessarily constitute aggression, but I'm not sure they feel extremely comfortable with it. This is why a strong, hard stare accompanied by "No! Bad dog!" is effective. It's a method they understand well. The alpha dog in a pack stares disapprovingly at actions he doesn't like, and soon enough, that behavior will stop. You are (or should be) the alpha dog in your "family pack."

When praising your dog, therefore, it's best to avoid a long stare. Look just a little to the side, especially at first, until your Basset thoroughly understands that you are not angry with him. In general, I keep long stares in reserve. Also, when scolding your dog, stand up straight and strong. Do not get down to his level. Our superior height (particularly effective where Bassets are concerned) is a major weapon in the discipline arsenal.

Bending over to scold your dog emulates the play-eliciting behavior of the dog world. You've seen it—the Basset crouches down in front and waggles his rear end, tail wagging furiously. Even if you don't waggle your rear, the Basset assumes that you're bending over him to invite him to play with you.

Will a Basset come when called?

Now it is certainly **possible** that your Basset Hound will actually come when called, but don't bank on it. More likely responses will be one of the following: (*a*) your Basset will pretend he doesn't hear you and continue doing whatever he was doing or (*b*) your Basset will stare at you appraisingly for a long moment, probably calculating as to whether it's worth his while to acquiesce, and then either (*b1*) rather grudgingly wander in your direction, (*b2*) turn his head away and stare vacantly into space, or (*b3*) run like hell in the other direction; some Bassets skip (*b*) altogether and go directly into (*b3*).

On the other hand, Melinda Brown's foster rescue dog, Chelsea, who is blind, passed the Canine Good Citizen test in May of 1996. This makes all three of Melinda's Bassets good citizens! (More than can be said for many people.) Melinda assures all of us that the CGC is "not difficult, really" and that the testers are "very lenient." She adds:

> If your dog is friendly with other dogs and people, and he knows to sit on command, you should be able to get him to pass. Using treats you can

get a Basset to do just about anything. And unlike an AKC trial, you can have the treats with you and you may use them to coax the dog to do the individual tests. They only have to sit long enough for you to walk 20 feet and return (about 15 seconds), and they just have to lie down on command—they don't have to stay.

The only other exercise that might be tricky is the recall. But here again, your dog only has to come when you call him from about 10 feet away, and you can call him as many times as you want. The Volhards' book, The Canine Good Citizen: Every Dog Can Be One, is a good reference.

Anita Wright says that her dogs could be obedient also, if they only wanted to.

Never ever call your dog for anything noxious like a bath or nail clipping. That will simply reinforce his natural disinclination to obey you when he has the slightest suspicion that it might not be a good idea. If you want to give the dog a bath, you'll have to go get him.

Always reward your Basset for doing what he's asked. Some may be satisfied with a pat or kind word, but most would really like a dog biscuit or piece of cheese. B.F. Skinner was right about some things.

My Basset puppy nips. How can I make him stop?

All puppies like to mouth and chew. It's the very nature of the critters. It's how they make friends. And with very young puppies (under 12 weeks), you may have to put up with some gentle nipping. That does not mean you have to encourage it. Pulling your hand away, although immediately effective, simply encourages the dog to try to "get it," and he'll probably lunge after you. He thinks it's a game. It's best to distract your Basset by offering a treat, or simply putting him away from you. Older puppies need to be dealt with more firmly—the long stare and "Bad dog!" routine work well.

Some people rely on coating their hand with some nasty smelling substance like Bitter Lemon. This may prevent the nipping problem, but it might foster a worse one—the Basset might decide your hand is the enemy and not even want to be petted! With consistent work, your young dog will learn the difference between playing and nipping. It's a little hard for him at first because in his litter, the standards were somewhat more lax.

Never allow your puppy to nip at you or anyone, even in play. This kind of behavior can escalate in a big hurry, and all of a sudden it's not funny anymore.

How can I teach my Basset Hound to howl?

The Basset Hound has the widest array of vocalizations of any of the dog breeds. Most Basset owners will certainly assert this to be true. Bassets not only bark in a variety of pitches, but they snore, grunt, moo, whine, mumble, and even make a strange, half-purring sound when their bellies are rubbed. But the strangest, most delightful, and spine-chilling of all Basset noises is their inimitable howl. In the old days, when Bassets were used more for hunting than they are today, a Basset would be included in nearly every hunting pack—even if the other dogs were Beagles or Foxhounds. The rich and musical tone of the Basset howl added an irreplaceable element.

In Basset circles, we say "bay," rather than howl, but it comes to the same thing. You may be surprised to know that one of the few characteristics the Basset has inherited from his wolf ancestors is that melodic, complex, and, to Basset lovers, eerily beautiful howl. Even one baying Basset sounds like a pack. (It has been noted by some, however, that the Basset howl never lasts more than 45 seconds, after which time it dies down. Of course, it may start up again immediately. I haven't timed this myself, but

Diane Morgan's Mugwump demonstrates just one of the Basset's possible vocalizations.

for those interested in such matters, it might be a good way to while away one's time—timing Basset bays.)

The origin of the term "bay" comes from the expression, "to bring to bay." My own Bassets have never brought anything to bay other than their supper dishes, however. You may have one dog, usually a male, who howls readily. This dog is called the "bell-hound" and may often be responsible for getting the others to howl as well. Our Miles is the bell-hound of our pack and has taught both Ruby and Mugwump to bay. Curiously enough, Miles is the bottom dog of our little pack. Ruby and Mugwump are still squabbling for alpha position, but **both** of them pick on poor Miles.

If you have no bell-hound in your pack, you may be reduced to getting down on your hands and knees and howling yourself, as an example. It's very critical to pull all the blinds down and lock the doors before performing this action. It's not something that can easily be explained to the neighbors.

Of course, Bassets have their own schedule for howling. It may not coincide with yours. Karla Miller tells us:

> Once a salesperson came to the door and looked at Mabel and remarked, "Oh, isn't she precious?" [Some people will say anything to make a sale.] At which point, as if on cue, Mabel started howling.

When our dear calico cat Maggie died, we buried her in our back meadow. Just as we were consigning her body to earth and her spirit to air, an eerie, mournful sound quavered on the air. It was our four Bassets, voicing in unison their sorrow at the departure of their longtime playmate and friend. It was a fitting tribute.

Can a Basset ever be trusted off the leash (or off-lead as we say snazzily in Basset circles)?

No. Not really. Inevitably, the hound nose will lead your Basset astray. Retrievers and such are oriented to their owners; they retrieve—that is, run and get what you've just shot. Bassets, on the other hand, were bred to independently sniff out game. This requires a degree of aplomb and self-possession simply out of reach for most dogs. Unfortunately, the Basset will soon be out of reach for you, too, so unless you are perfectly willing to spend several hours floundering about in the bushes yelling hoarsely for your Basset, keep him on a leash.

Here is a tale from Will Mack, who owns two Bassets, Becky and Dasher. He enrolled both of them in a set of 10-week obedience classes, and they were **perfect** in the yard at home. The day came when at class they were to be off-lead for the first time:

> *Becky was heeling beautifully for about 50 feet, when she decided she wanted to go and visit Dasher and bolted across the lawn, ignoring my calls to get her attention. She was clearly ignoring me. Once she got back to Dasher, they started to roll around and play, expecting me, when I arrived red-faced and puffing, to join in the game. I thought to try Dasher on the off-lead exercise, since Becky clearly wasn't in the mood. As I took the lead off Dasher's collar, a flock of swallows came swooping in about four feet off the ground. Becky, who has a fascination with birds, took off after them with Dasher in pursuit. They charged through an opening in a stone wall and followed the birds to the edge of the road, where they miraculously stopped, and turned, heading back to me. They arrived a minute or two later.*

> *I was quite pleased at how they were coming right back to me, when a jogger came around a tree and headed for the tennis courts. The Bassets took off after him at top speed. They couldn't quite catch him, though, and stayed about two feet behind. The jogger looked a little nervous with two hounds at his heels, but he was apparently confident he could easily outrun them.*

By the time William caught his beasts, he vowed never to take their leashes off again, even while they were sleeping. Some things are just too much of a temptation, even for a dog who likes very much to obey.

As an epilogue to this story, it is nice to know that Becky and Dasher both eventually received their CD (Companion Dog) certificates. Some things are just too much of a temptation, even for a dog who likes very much to obey.

Sometimes, of course, Bassets want even more contact with their owners than a leash provides. Neil Hammond writes:

> One night recently we were taking Daisy for a walk. She was fine as long as there was some light. We decided to cross an open, unlighted area as a shortcut, and Daisy dug in her heels. She simply would not go any farther, and no amount of coaxing could make her go. I had to **carry** her across this field until we had reached a lighted area. This is not the first time she has balked at walking in the dark areas. I think she is afraid of the dark.

Neil is wrong, of course. Daisy is not afraid of the dark. She's merely concerned about what might be **in** the dark, waiting to grab her. Very sensible, in my opinion.

So, Bassets are good hunters, aren't they?

Yes, although they cannot catch anything. Well, that's not precisely true. They are very good at picking up all sorts of dead and rotting things and then eating them. They are also clever at bothering skunks. Other trophies Bassets have brought back from their woodland rambles include: antlers (no deer attached), empty cans of Hormel chili, and something that looked like mummy wrappings.

Our Mugwump once disappeared into the woods on a search-and-destroy mission and came trotting proudly back, bearing a toilet seat in her jaws.

An effective hunting posture: Judy Trenck's Big Girl lying in wait.

Can I teach my Basset to sit still for photos?

When this question popped up on our newsgroup, someone contributed an anonymous set of instructions on how to photograph a puppy. I was unable to trace the letter back to its original author, but I have decided to include it anyway—for its priceless insight into the canine (and human) mind-set. This version came from Kitty Nodsle:

1. Remove film from box and load camera.
2. Remove box from puppy's mouth and throw in trash bin.
3. Retrieve puppy from trash bin and brush coffee grounds from muzzle.
4. Choose a suitable background for photo.
5. Mount camera on tripod and focus.
6. Find puppy and take dirty sock from mouth.
7. Place puppy in prefocused spot and return to camera.
8. Forget about spot and crawl after puppy on hands and knees.
9. Focus with one hand and fend off puppy with other hand.

The best solution to the puppy photo problem may be to get a professional. This portrait of Julius and Linda Curley's Elvis is proof that these people know what they're doing.

10. Get tissue and clean off nose print from lens.
11. Take flash cube from puppy's mouth and throw in trash bin.
12. Put cat outside and apply peroxide to scratch on puppy's nose.
13. Put magazines back on coffee table.
14. Try to get puppy's attention by squeaking toy over your head.
15. Replace your glasses and check camera for damage.

16. Jump up in time to grab puppy by scruff of neck and say, "No!! Outside!!! No, outside!"

17. Call spouse to clean up mess.

18. Fix a drink. Make it a double.

19. Sit back in recliner and resolve to train puppy to "Sit" and "Stay" first thing in the morning.

When challenged to come up with a real solution to the doggie-sit-still problem, I admit to being stumped. The problem boils down to this: If you're close enough to take a picture, the dog will want to amble over and see what you're doing. However, I do have some suggestions:

1. Photograph said dog while he is asleep or drugged.

2. Take him to a pet photographer. There's a reason why pet photographers are in this business. They know what they're doing.

3. Use a telephoto lens. Of course, if you're enough of a photographer to have a telephoto lens, you already know this. The following picture of Mugwump was taken from a distance of approximately 25 feet with a zoom telephoto extended to about 200 mm.

A telephoto lens may allow you to photograph your dog while he's not paying attention. (Mugwump, Diane Morgan)

4. Try to take the dog's photo when he's interested in something else—like chewing your underwear. Makes for a cute snapshot, too.

5. Have plenty of film and patience. Be ready to take many, many photos before you get one suitable enough for the family scrapbook. But keep trying.

How smart is a Basset?

Much smarter than most dogs. Let's face it, most dogs belong in the "dim bulb" category—running around and fetching your paper and slippers, rolling over on command, and sticking by your side through all sorts of distractions. Not a Basset. Bassets are too smart to do a lot of tricks, for instance, and smart enough to make you a slave to their whims. Most people confuse high intelligence with "trainability," a quality that Poodles and Labradors, for instance, have in abundance. Labradors lie around the house waiting to be told what to do.

We basseteers know that our dogs are **far too intelligent** to perform a bunch of slavish antics at our command, although they are quite ready to do them when one is least expecting them. My Mugwump, for example, is particularly adept at climbing up on the kitchen table, eating everything on it—from doughnuts to watches—**very silently,** and, when done, whining politely to be hoisted down from the table. (Bassets, by the way, must be hoisted. Simple lifting won't do the trick.)

Basset Hounds are just about as smart as they need to be in any given situation. For example, a story from Anne Whitacre:

Some Bassets are so intelligent they can read upside down. (Duchess, Beth Hinchliffe)

Esther has picked up a couple of new tricks. She now takes her leash down from the hook and rattles it around so that I get the idea about taking her for a walk. And she has learned to turn off the space heater with her paw. I have this space heater in my office, and Esther likes to sleep in front of it. When she gets too warm, she just takes her paw and shuts it off.

Mugwump is particularly adept at climbing on the kitchen table and devouring everything on it.

Karen Fetter tells the following about her friend's Basset Hound, Ramona Lisa:

> [She] grabbed the remote control from her human dad, Bob, while he was eating his burger. (Bob is no lightweight.) Mona ran out the doggie door with the remote, and Bob came chasing after her. She tossed the remote behind the house in the brush. Bob, loving both his food and his TV remote, set off to retrieve the remote in the brush while Mona ran in the house and ate his hamburger.

So Bassets cannot be taught to do tricks?

This is not quite true. I have a friend of a friend who taught her Basset, Natasha, to yawn on command. That's about it. No, wait! JoAnne Smith says her Basset, Earl, will sit up straight and stick his tongue out on command. Pretty impressive.

As far as conventional tricks like run and fetch, roll over and play dead, and jump through hoops, give up. The Bassets, however, will watch you with interest for hours, while you, the superior being, fetch and carry, roll over, and so on. Then, they'll go to sleep. Who's the smart one?

My Basset is terrified of thunderstorms. What's the cure?

About 23.5 percent of Bassets go ga-ga during a thunderstorm. Since this number equals the degree of inclination of the earth's axis, there is probably a connection somewhere. If you have the misfortune to be owned by a storm-fearer, you have several options. None of these may actually work, but you can try them:

1. *Ignore the whole thing.* Pretend that your hound isn't really cowering and moaning under the couch because the barometric pressure has dropped one or two millimeters. The advantage of this system is that by an admirable degree of self-deception, you can avoid doing anything complicated or expensive. On the downside, you do realize that you must cancel all appointments and family and career plans while you baby-sit your terrified dog. Tell everyone that your Basset is very ill and needs to be nursed. Obviously you can't tell people the truth. It sounds ridiculous.

2. *Try desensitizing your dog to storms.* This will only work if you are not the teeniest-weeniest bit afraid of thunderstorms yourself. If you are, the dog can *smell* it on you. (No kidding—you're giving off a scent signal that says, "Run and hide, the sky is falling!") If you are fearless, you must speak cheerfully and gaily to your pet: "Oh, boy, look! A nice *thunderstorm!* Isn't this *fun?* How would you like a nice, big old dog biscuit? Let's *play a game!*" Do not attempt to hold or comfort your pet. This will only confirm in him the suspicion that there is, indeed, something very much wrong. You may even want to play records of storms. Of course, you don't actually want to go *out* and run around with your Basset Hound in a *real* thunderstorm. They're dangerous, something your hound has been trying to tell you all this time.

   If your dog is afraid of vacuum cleaners also (this applies to about 75 percent of all storm-fearing Bassets), you might want to start with desensitizing your pet to them. It's easier.

Curing thunderstorm-phobia is *not* easy. To be honest, I've never heard of a case that I consider really cured. After all, thunderstorms are really deadly manifestations of nature's tremendous powers, and in their ancestral wolf days, all sensible creatures took cover during a storm. Your dog's genetics are speaking strongly to him. It's hard to argue with that.

3. *Drug your Basset.* Although I do not normally recommend drugging dogs, if your Basset is truly terrified of storms, and your vet agrees, a little valium or other tranquilizer (using the correct dosage recommended for your dog) administered when the barometric pressure starts to drop may be helpful. It may also work to desensitize your dog gradually to thunderstorms, and he may eventually grow out of his fear.

How many Bassets make a herd, or baggle, of Bassets?

One.

How can anyone resist the Basset's soulful eyes?

Tea at 4:00? Of course!

Barbados Basset

Art imitates life!

Ah, the stories I could tell about my roaming adventures. . .

Let's go! Mardi Gras is calling my name!

A Times Square frolic!

The Basset's regal countenance.

Dog Shows and Related Beastly Events

Can Bassets be trained in obedience?

The first thing to remember is that Basset Hounds do not obey. They may acquiesce. But as Chris Wallen, who writes the "Obedience Column" for *Tally Ho*, the Basset Hound Club of America newsletter, writes: "If we didn't like challenges, we'd be training Shelties!"

If you're looking for a by-the-numbers, robotic obedience dog, forget about Bassets; try one of the obedience breeds like Labradors. This is not to say a Basset Hound cannot do well in obedience training. Let's just say it's . . . unusual. A Basset **may** decide, as a particular favor, on a particular day—perhaps your birthday—to surprise you and trot cheerfully around the ring at your heel, doing everything you ask. All I'm saying is don't count on it.

Still, it doesn't hurt to make the attempt. All AKC-sponsored obedience events require that your dog be purebred, but he can be neutered, which is not the case with conformation-type shows. Four titles, indicative of ascending achievement, are possible: CD (Companion Dog), CDX (Companion Dog Excellent), UD (Utility Dog), and UDX (Utility Dog Excellent). It must be stated that very few Bassets make it to the UD level,

Nellie, (Belinda Lanphear)

and only a very, very few make it to the top CDX tier. You should consider this a challenge.

Melinda Brown entered her Basset, BOW, in the heel free exercise at the Old Dominion Kennel Club match. The indoor ring had been set up so that it was just a few feet away from the judges' lunch kitchen. During the class, Melinda did very well, following the correct route with no mistakes whatever. BOW, on the other hand, turned right instead of left—right into the kitchen. Although this disqualified BOW, I feel that any self-respecting Basset would do the same. What's the point in following one's deranged owner, who is walking around in circles for no apparent reason, especially when there is food to be had? Unfortunately for BOW, he was quickly returned to his disgruntled owner without so much as a cheeseburger for his troubles.

For BOW and Melinda Brown, obedience training has been challenging and rewarding.

Still, as Melinda writes:

> Obedience training isn't for everyone or for every Basset. It's a lot of hard work. But it allows the dog and owner to forge a much deeper, richer relationship! Dogs, and Bassets in particular, love attention, and one thing that happens when you are doing obedience is that your dog gets your undivided attention. I've been seriously working for about a year on getting a CD with BOW. But I've been doing obedience work with him since we got him about two years ago. We started because he needed attention in a structured environment. He was a basket case— hence his name, BOW (Bounces Off Walls). But with the obedience training he got perspective and saw that we cared for him by taking the time to work with him daily and teach him things. BOW was a quick

study, eager to learn and please. Now he is my closest companion next to my husband. We have a bond that will never break, no matter what happens in the ring.

Bow has since received his CD.

Not everyone is so lucky. Sue Lockhart says:

Just before we were called into the show ring, I was trying to wipe the slobber off Sophie's face [a perennial problem with Bassets] when she grabbed the towel thinking we were going to play tug. She refused to let go, and I ended up leading her into the ring by a towel. We lost.

Jeanne McBride writes:

I enrolled Cleo into an eight-week obedience course. I had visions of graduating with a dog that would sit, stay, and lie down on command, a dog that would not pull your arm out of the socket. Here are some examples of what actually happened: The down command. Cleo would never go down the same way twice. Probably she figured that since she had already done it once, she might as well try for a little variety. Sometimes her fore end would go down first, sometimes her aft. Sometimes she would throw all legs out at once in all directions and lay her head completely down on one side, while she puffed her lips out and sighed heavily. The instructor shook her head.

Some people have no sense of humor.

Jennifer Beezley is currently not speaking to her husband in regard to this issue:

I told him I was going to work with Lucy and register her in obedience trials. He laughed and said he didn't think there was a category for "fastest rollover for a belly rub" or a "chase the sock" category!

Jonathan Silverman adds:

I've only seen a Basset in an obedience trial once, a few years ago at the huge annual dog show at McCormick Place in Chicago. Based on our own Basset's interest in obedience, my wife and I were prepared to be amazed. We weren't. The dog wouldn't even come when called. (This was in front of a hundred or so onlookers; I felt sorry for the owner.) My conclusion: Some dogs are born to obey, some to rule.

As mentioned in Chapter 5, I did hear of a Basset Hound, named Natasha, who was trained to yawn on command, but I don't believe that is a recognized event at most obedience trials.

Lis Fieldman has some suggestions for obedience trials more appropriately geared to the natural abilities of the Basset Hound:

> *The Stop and Smell the Roses Maneuver: To demonstrate the hound's natural resistance to traveling in a straight line, the Basset must display excellent dawdling technique while being moved from Point A to Point B. (Bassets making an actual attempt to get to Point B under their own willpower are disqualified.) Points can be scored by the number of blades of grass that are individually examined, the number of far-off sounds heard and responded to, and, of course, the number of times the hound walks off in completely the wrong direction. Bonus points to be awarded if the Basset falls asleep during the event.*

> *The Bath Day Bash: To demonstrate the Basset's ability to hear running water, correctly assume that it's bath time, and escape. Points to be awarded on bath avoidance techniques such as running away, incessant howling, or faking a coma. Bonus points to be awarded to the hound who can hide until the owner has given up.*

What about field trials?

The earliest brace (in dog talk, a brace is two dogs) field trials began with the Basset Hound Club of America in 1937. Trials are generally held in the spring and fall. My Basset Hound club held a field trial this spring, and so, as part of my research for this book, I went. The trials were held at a Beagle club, which I understand is the general rule (as there appear to be more beaglers than basseteers), except for a Basset club in Ohio, which has its own grounds. Training for novice dogs was to be held afterwards, so I brought along our Ruby, the best noser of our three Bassets. Ruby would actually be ineligible for anything sponsored by the AKC, since she: (a) is spayed and (b) has no papers because she is a rescue dog. But I have never held either of these two things against her personally, so I brought her along.

As we trundled up the hill to where the trials were being held, I heard some shouting and saw a lot of waving hands. It turned out the shouting was directed at us. "Stop! Stop!" cried everyone urgently. "You'll cross the rabbit track!" These words did, in fact, stop me cold.

When, after a few minutes, I was permitted to join the rest of the group (who turned out to be some of the most friendly and down-to-earth folks I've ever met), I managed to ask nervously, "Rabbit? What rabbit? We're not out here to kill any little BUNNY RABBITS, are we?" (I was probably shouting at this point.) Ruby looked around happily.

"Are you kidding? Bassets can't catch rabbits. The rabbits are too quick. We're here to **trail** the rabbits."

"Aha," said I, nodding wisely. "Trail the rabbits. I see." I was later relieved to learn that rabbits are never killed at field trials, not even at gun trials.

So began a day of struggling through a couple hundred acres of tick-infested bushes (which for some reason we beat with sticks). Every once in a while, someone would cry out, "tally ho!" (really), and a rabbit would dart out of the bushes and sit down. The field Bassets would smell it and, when they got a good whiff, begin to bark (or give voice, as they say). Then off we'd all go after the rabbit. The rabbits, who were used to eluding the Bassets' more enterprising and adroit cousins, the Beagles,

"Look Fred, a duck! Two of 'em!"

apparently thought this was all great fun. They spent the morning dashing in and out of the bushes like mad. Sometimes they'd wait for the Bassets to catch up before zooming off again in a different direction.

The field trial dogs were quite impressive, actually, and I heard tell of one Basset who was a five-time champion—and blind. Ruby had an excellent time; she flushed out a few rabbits and chased them—silently, I'm afraid. Another disqualification.

My favorite novice dog at the trials, however, was Caruso, owned by Nancy Gallagher. Caruso is a dignified and portly Basset of middle years. He took one look at the other Bassets charging madly about in all directions seeking rabbits and promptly trampled down a nice, soft, comfortable spot in the long grass where he went to sleep. Nancy urged her noble hound to join in the fun, but Caruso gave her a look as if to say, "If you want to get hot and sweaty chasing rabbits around the puckerbrush, go right ahead. Leave me out of it." He showed uncommonly good sense, I thought. Nancy told me later that "the only thing he managed to sniff out that day was a large barrel with what looked suspiciously like rabbit food inside."

Using his innate Basset talents, Amanda Sherwin's Peabody hunts swans.

Anita Wright comments:

My husband nearly fell off his chair laughing at the thought of Watson being a member of a hunting pack of trained dogs. He says the only trials Watson could be doing would be mattress trials.

This was in response to Watson's (a refugee from an animal shelter) strange and hitherto unidentified tattoos; it was suggested that tattoos in more than one place might indicate that he had at one time been a member of a hunting pack.

Can Bassets track?

It's what they are bred for! The American Kennel Club offers two tracking titles—TD (Tracking Dog) and TDX (Tracking Dog Excellent)—awarded to dogs who can successfully sniff out lost or hidden objects, usually a glove. (Since the O.J. Simpson case, though, some competitors have wanted to switch to something less incriminating.) The dogs would prefer looking for food, actually.

Mind you, tracking is not for the faint of heart. It requires a highly dedicated Basset-human pair who is willing to put in long hours of practice. At the present time, not nearly enough Bassets compete in this event, which is too bad. It should be their forte.

Are Bassets agile?

Well, let's face it. No. But they can be fun to show in agility contests anyway. Patty Nordstrom and Smuckers attempted this and had a blast. Smuckers was the only Basset there:

> Smuckers had no problem with the jumps, serpentine, ramps, seesaw, or sit-stay. But there was no way she would go through the tunnels. Even with me at one end with a treat and someone else at the other end pushing. . . . After the trials I don't know how many people came up and said how much they enjoyed watching Smuckers and what a nice dog she was.

Even at home, they aren't really anything to brag about. Beth Hinchliffe has this story to tell about her late and splendid Duchess:

> Once my dad and I were out for the afternoon and came home to find her trapped between the chair and the wall. She had apparently nosed her

Karen Clemente's Ashley demonstrates sheer Basset agility.

way in to change the radio station—the only thing behind the chair is the stereo. She had about two inches of clearance on each side, but could no more gracefully back out of that Basset-sized prison than she could sprout wings and fly to freedom. We came home to the most pathetic sight. There was no room for her to lie down. Her nose and tail had drooped to the floor—we could only guess how long she'd been waiting! And, of course, she was mumbling self-pityingly to herself. It took roughly a second and a half to grasp the compliant rear end and lead her back a few inches to freedom. Then, of course, the Basset Face for the rest of the day.

For those who have a spirit of adventure, though, agility trials are wonderful excursions into a zany world. The first "agility trial" was held in 1978 at the Crufts International Dog Show. (This is one of the world's largest and most prestigious dog shows, by the way, putting our own Westminster Dog Show to shame both in number of dogs exhibited and number of events judged.) Today, in the United States, all recognized agility trials are held under the auspices of the United States Dog Agility Association (USDAA). The object of the event is for your precious Basset to negotiate a series of obstacles, including a tunnel, a seesaw, numerous jumps, A-frame ramps, and other ingenious devices. The dog who gets through cleanly in the shortest time is the winner. The dog must also show at least the rudiments of obedience by sitting or lying down for a five-second count. Jumps are lowered or raised according to the height of the dog, so Bassets are not penalized for being short.

Dogs compete regardless of breed, so it's not unusual to see a Poodle against a Great Dane, or a Weimeraner versus a Sheepdog. It's true that Border Collies usually win this event, but Bassets are the darlings of the crowd every time. We had a Basset who did extremely well in all aspects of the event, although he did take his time sniffing carefully through the tunnel. It was the obedience part that marked his downfall.

This stuff sounds too hard.
Is there anything easier?

Of course there is! Just made for Bassets is the Canine Good Citizen test. And who would prefer a "utility dog" for a pet over a Canine Good Citizen? The Canine Good Citizen test is **noncompetitive!** Everyone can win. To get your dog this valuable certificate, he needs to be able to do the following things:

1. **Accept a friendly stranger.** This is a snap for any self-respecting hound. Bassets enjoy meeting people, but they don't tend to go ga-ga over them. Further, no points are taken off for soaking said stranger's hand in Basset drool, although it must be admitted that in real life, friendly strangers can become considerably less friendly after such an experience. They often ask you if there is something wrong with your dog. (You could answer mischievously, "Aside from the rabies, no.")

2. **Sit politely for petting.** Bassets are good at this also. They love to be petted. The only problem is that the Basset will likely roll over for a belly rub while being petted. An indulgent judge, however, should understand that for Bassets, this is as polite as can be.

3. **Appearance and grooming.** The Basset must allow his paws to be picked up, his coat to be brushed, and his ears to be lifted and peered into without objection. Don't embarrass yourself here. Make sure everything is up to par with your Basset, including the dreaded nail trimming and ear cleaning.

4. **Walk on a loose leash.** If your Basset pulls, you might be in for trouble, so practice first. Mind you, the dog does not need to heel like a robot, but he shouldn't be dragging you all over the place either.

5. **Walk through a crowd.** The organizers of the event will have a bunch of patsies who stand and mill around and pretend to be a crowd. No Basset is ever fooled by this and will march through this part of the trial with aplomb.

6. **Sit and stay.** Uh-oh. It's always something, isn't it? This is the downfall of most Bassets. If your Basset sits, he may not stay. Or he may not get up (next test). He may not sit in the first place. Try begging.

7. **Come when called.** Even if your Basset will get up, he may not come to you, but find a more interesting person to waddle over to. The test allows you to use body language to get the dog to come, and I must say I've seen some **very** interesting body language at this stage of the test.

8. **Reaction to another dog.** Here the Basset must show polite indifference toward meeting one of his own kind. If he bites the other dog in the face, he will not pass, and that's that. Practice this stage carefully at home.

9. **Reaction to distractions.** This is always a fun part of the test. At one event I attended, one of the sponsors kept throwing lawn chairs around. None of the dogs paid the slightest attention to this aberrant behavior, but one of the humans I was with leaned over and asked me in a worried voice, "Why is that guy throwing chairs?" The kind of distractions is left up to the sponsors of the event and can indeed be very creative. Bassets do well in this stage, as long as the distraction is not edible. Then you're sunk.

10. **Supervised separation.** You must leave your Basset under the care of someone else while you walk out of sight. Most Bassets use this as an opportunity to go to sleep, which is allowable. And preferable, from the Basset's point of view.

Your Basset must pass each leg of the test to get his Canine Good Citizen certificate, suitable for framing. While not actually worth anything, it should provide you with a sense of pride and achievement for your dog. As for the Basset, he couldn't care less.

Fun shows

These are my favorite kind—no pressure (and no points) and no money to be gained, except for the charity that's running them. A couple of my favorites from around the country are as follows.

The Great Michigan Basset Waddle

In 1996, the Waddle made $11,500 for Bassets and Michigan Basset Rescue. Miss Xanadu made a shocking debut in her gold and pink. *Life* magazine showed up at the Michigan Waddle, and as JoAnne Smith wrote:

> *The photographers tried to get a group picture of all 200 Bassets off-lead. They tried herding them into a group, using people as a human fence. The Bassets had no idea what was going on, so they just sat facing their humans. Cameras got shots of lots of Basset rumps. Some Bassets escaped. Finally, the photographers just lined them up in front of the lake—on leashes—with their humans. I'll bet the photographers learned something about the Basset mind that day.*

Unfortunately, the Basset Waddle photos did not make the cut at *Life*. The editors instead decided to do a profile of a bullfight and included a lovely shot of a dead bull. I'm happy to report, though, that *Life* did run the piece—a year late, but just in time for the May 1997 Waddle.

The 1997 Waddle was indeed a thrilling event, one which had to be seen to be believed. Six hundred fat Bassets ambled down the main street, crammed in between a high school marching band and the King and Queen Basset Float. For some odd reason, people along the parade route often burst into unaccountable **laughter** upon seeing the Bassets, almost as if there were something odd about the whole thing. Odd or not, in 1997, we raised $30,000 for Michigan Bassets, enough to give every homeless hound in the state a condominium and cable.

On a more serious note, Michigan Basset Rescue is probably the premier dog rescue organization in the country and generously donates thousands of dollars every year to help Bassets all across the country—everything from glaucoma operations to hydrotherapy.

"Waddle On!"

A friend of mine in Doberman Rescue (now there's a risky hobby) wondered if perhaps they couldn't organize a Doberman Walk. I don't know. Somehow I think the sight of 600 Dobermans walking down the main street might produce a different effect. The spectators might run.

Woodinville (Washington) Basset Bash

The day begins with the annual Basset Brigade, part of the All Fools Day Parade. The Brigade features about 300 Basset buddies leading their hapless human subjects down Woodinville's world-famous thoroughfare. Beginning about 1:30 P.M., the Basset Bash drags on until approximately 4:00 when the vertically challenged dogs fiercely compete (between naps) for Best Howl, Best Waddle, Best Trick, Longest Ears, Funniest Name, Oldest Dog, Greatest Distance Traveled, and Most Original Costume awards. Finally, the Great Wienie Race is run, and the King and Queen Basset are crowned.

Let's face it. No one knows how to have fun like Basset owners.

The Annual Basset Olympics

The Basset Olympics are held in Lebanon, Oregon. Events include: a Parade of Rescue Dogs, the 11-Yard Puppy Dash, a Dancing Contest (solo or pairs), Synchronized Swimming, Basset Bingo, the Basset Decathlon, and awards for Best Tail Wagger, Best Trick, Best Costume, Endurance Sitting, Longest Ears, Basset-Child Look-Alike, and Best Howler. There is also a People's Choice Photo Award. No sled dog competition is offered, which is too bad, for I'm sure Bassets would be excellent sledders, if only you could line up enough of them. And get them to move forward. In the same direction. At the same time.

This is a fund-raiser held for the EEBHF (Emerald Empire Basset Hound Fanciers) Rescue Fund.

Is my dog a candidate for therapy?

Well, that depends on what you mean. Of course, there are dog psychiatrists, dog psychologists, and animal communicators, but what I'm referring to here is using your Basset as a therapy for others: people in nursing homes, homebound children, and so on. If your Basset is quiet and friendly (has he passed his Good Citizen test?), you may like to perform a little community service by sharing the pleasure of his company with others. Contact your local ASPCA and see about joining a pet therapy class. The rewards will be endless, for all concerned.

SEVEN

The Beast Feasts:
Your Basset's Diet

What do Bassets eat?

This is a frightening question.

Most books on dogs will tell you what to feed your dogs, so there's no use whatever in going over **that** here. This section, however, will enlighten you as to what Bassets really do eat. As you will discover in the course of this chapter, among the multiple graces of the Basset Hound is the capacity to devour, if not to completely digest, any and all objects within the range of his eyes or nose.

First, however, I am providing a sample menu for a Basset over the course of a day:

Breakfast: Preferred entree—steak and eggs (any style), ham, and sausage. No ketchup on the eggs. Will settle for—dog food and burnt toast. Prefers butter on toast, but will eat it dry.

Mid-morning snack: Preferred entree—hamburger scrounged from the counter. Likes the hamburger defrosted, but this is not absolutely necessary. Will settle for—dog biscuit or slice of apple or carrot.

Lunch: Preferred entree—leftover stew or lasagna from previous night. Also leftover macaroni and cheese. Or a bologna sandwich. Or a hamburger. Will settle for—a bite of anything that you're eating.

High tea at the Basset House

Mid-afternoon snack: Preferred entree—large hunks of cheddar cheese or leftover cat food. Will settle for—just about anything.

High tea: Preferred entree—large number of cupcakes and cookies, delicate ladyfingers, and cucumber sandwiches. Does not require tea. Will settle for—contents of trash can.

Supper: Preferred entree—slices of roast beef or turkey breast, mashed or baked potatoes, and mixed vegetables. Will settle for—dog food spiced up with remainders of above.

Evening television snack: Preferred entree—leftovers from supper, described above. Will settle for—dropped pieces of popcorn.

Late-night refrigerator raid: Preferred entree—a true Dagwood sandwich with all the fixings. Will settle for—any remains of the same, which guilt-ridden human gives Basset to silence him for fear of waking spouse and incurring reprisals about breaking diet regimen.

I asked the members of my newsgroup to send me lists of things their dogs have actually devoured (and in some cases digested). I'm passing this list along to you. On the whole, it seems that the most popular items include feces (of any species), dirty underwear (especially underwear with crotches), socks, nylons (panty hose with crotch preferred), and disposable razors. Most Bassets also eat soap (some unwrap the bars first), toilet paper and tissue, and eyeglasses—they have a definite preference for designer brands. Other occasional delicacies include:

Aluminum foil

Ants

Birth control pills (human—
    entire month's supply)

Bugs (assorted species)

Carpet fibers and patches
    (oriental preferred)

Chocolate fudge cake (whole,
    with packaging)

Cicadas (live preferred)

Christmas cactus

Christmas tree lights

Christmas tree ornaments

Dirt

Earphones

Eggshells

Ferns

Fish heads

Flag

Grapefruit skins

Grass (thrown up later)
Half of a dead duck
Hearing aid
Hornet's nest (empty)
Ice cubes
Italian leather wallet (expensive)
Jewelry
Kid gloves (liners left for owner)
Kite string
Kleenex
Legos
Money (various denominations, see below)
Mud
Nails
Okra
Pencils and pens
Plush penguin
Pom-poms
Quartz watch
Radishes (by the bag)
Rocks
Shoes (Hush Puppies, naturally)
Squeakers from dog toys
Steak (stolen from the table and not intended for Basset)
Sunflower seeds
Tulips
TV remotes (a popular item)
Urine-soaked diapers
Velcro
Vomit (any kind)
Worms
X-rays (human—dental)
Wrigley Field Cubs cap (official version)
Zippers

In case your Basset should accidentally, or, as is more probable, intentionally, swallow some disgusting and unhealthy object, call your veterinarian immediately. If you know what the object was, and the vet recommends that you make your dog vomit, you can pour a requisite amount of ipecac down his Basset throat. If you don't have any (and it is something you should keep handy), you can use about one tablespoon of hydrogen peroxide to make him vomit the loathsome object. Hydrogen peroxide works fast—in about two minutes. You might want to give it to him outside. It should be noted that hydrogen peroxide, while not poisonous in reasonable doses, is harsh on the stomach. Expect your Basset to be uncomfortable for a while afterwards. Digel is also useful to keep on hand. It may protect your Basset from bloat, one of the most frightening and serious conditions that can occur.

A charming tale comes from Gretchen Laffert, who is owned by the stunning Miss Xanadu:

Xanadu was ill for approximately seven weeks with some strange "something." I had had her to the vet about four times because of her vomiting and lack of appetite, but I never received a specific diagnosis. Then, one evening when I got home from work, I noticed a bulge on the side of her abdomen—and an uncomfortable looking dog. "Oh, no," I thought, "the big C." The very next morning, while on the phone with my vet to get X-rays, my husband called for me to come outside. Something was wrong with Xanadu. I ran outside, and, to my absolute amazement, I saw something extending for about 15 inches from her rectum. It was ugly, smelly, flat, and about one and a half inches wide. At first, I thought it was some type of worm and dragged her to the vet— with the "thing" dragging behind. The vet came into the examining room and said, "Hmm, that's interesting," and began pulling. Out came my son's necktie. It was in perfect condition—no rips or chewed ends. In fact, even the label was still intact.

Gretchen does not report as to whether the tie was worn again by her son.

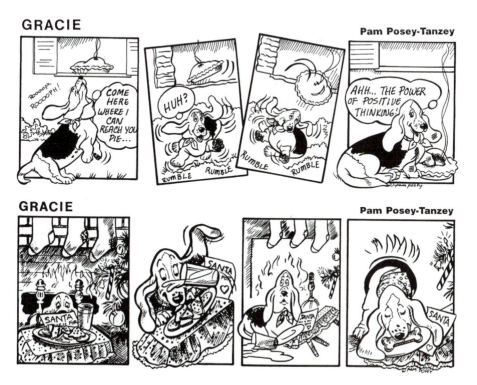

If ties are not acceptable Basset food, then what is? If you are feeding your pet commercial food, make sure that it carries the AAFCO (Association of American Feed Control Officials) approval seal. Look for food that is high in animal crude protein. This kind of protein, as opposed to the vegetable sort, is easy to digest, provides lots of energy, and results in less smelly dog droppings (always an important consideration). Dogs are by nature carnivores, not vegetarians. Vegetables may be profitably added to a diet, but your dog subsists primarily on meat. If your dog is stressed out, add even more protein to his diet. It helps.

Some people like to give their pets a home-cooked diet. This is wonderful if you have the time and you take care to provide all the essential nutrients. Homemade diets are particularly important if your dog suffers from allergies or has special nutritional needs. Several books on the subject are available. Do not attempt this, however, unless you're sure that you know what you're doing!

Jeanne McBride tells us:

> Cleo is a vegetarian. She especially loves potatoes. We also have berry-producing trees in the yard, and every day she goes out and inspects her trees. If there is ripe fruit available, Cleo will gently harvest the fruit with her mouth. She has also raided the tomato and pepper plants. Once she ate a basil plant that literally turned her green. She smelled somewhat like a pickle afterwards.

Nancy Gallagher's Caruso favors potatoes also—in the Lay's Sour Cream and Onion variety. He keeps his stash behind the couch.

Another favorite story came from Jane Holeywell about her prior Basset, Spot (Jane's husband is named Richard, so what can you expect?):

> Spot delighted in eating my toddler daughter's Crayola crayons. Do you remember the **REALLY BIG** box of about 84 crayons, the one with the built-in sharpener on the back? Imagine the crayons making their nontoxic way through the Basset digestive track . . . imagine the Technicolor poop in my backyard. It was the talk of the neighborhood.

Debra Kozik's dogs, Sneakers and Trooper, are devil-may-care Twizzler thieves.

Along frighteningly similar lines is Bill and Debbie Kozik's experience:

> When I was outside taking care of my plants and flowers, Trooper decided to get onto the kitchen table and steal the Twizzlers that were on it. (My other Basset, Sneakers, is too short to reach the table.) However, Sneakers must have stolen them from Trooper, because when I walked back into the house, there was Sneakers, lying in the middle of the living room with an empty two-pound Twizzlers wrapper close by. I checked doggie breath and teeth, and, sure enough, Sneakers had Twizzler breath and red teeth. The following day, he also had red poop.

And a page from the diary of Ms. Molly, companion of Bill James:

> Doing my bit to help clean up the Christmas decorations got me busted again! The Bearded One was just sitting there quietly, doing nothing more tiring than simple respiration, contemplating the insides of his eyelids. Mrs. TBO was carefully wrapping the lights, ornaments, and all that other no-no stuff. When she went out on the front porch, I quietly

climbed up on the sofa (another no-no), gracefully leapt to the top of the coffee table (also prohibited), and shoved a whole dish of Hershey's Kisses onto the floor—a very major infraction of the rules! Yet, no one was the wiser.

Mustering all my somewhat limited self-control, I managed to keep Bosley and ClioPatra safe from all that candy, as I know that it can make them sick. Sacrificially throwing myself on this chocolate grenade to protect my pals, I swiftly gobbled up all but the last two pieces myself. I then backed off the remaining candy (I know my limits), allowed the other dogs to help themselves, and began barking reproachfully. It worked! TBO awoke, and Bosley and ClioPatra got a swift ticket to the backyard. What a plan. I got ear massages and tummy rubs for pointing out their misbehavior to TBO. (The tummy rubs felt great, as I was feeling a little queasy from all that chocolate.)

The next morning in the yard, TBO was tending to our fruit trees when nature called me. Carefree, and with no pangs of conscience from the day before, I did my duty. TBO, who was holding the water hose, decided to wash my contribution into the grass as he is kind of cheap that way regarding fertilizer. The high pressure hose yielded a "AHA!! Molly, what is this?" I tried to tell him the obvious, that it was dog poop and nothing but, but the bright Christmas colors of the Kisses wrappers gave it all away. ClioPatra and Bosley were inside the rest of the day with extra Milk Bones. I staffed the back porch until after dark. Next year, I must figure out how to unwrap the goodies using these big paws with no opposable thumbs.

Lynn Herf writes:

My Basset, Megan, has eaten 30 pennies at one time. She threw up some, and we found the rest gradually as we cleaned the yard. Also, one time I received a package from Germany with cookies and chocolates. We had the front gate locked so the mail carrier must have set it on top of the newspaper box. We didn't see it when we got home, so we let the dogs out. I looked outside and saw that they had torn the box open and were eating the cookies. I think I salvaged a couple of chocolates.

Later on, Megan expanded her eating repertoire to drywall. She actually ate a hole in the wall, perhaps looking for a place to hide any future pennies devoured. After a couple of X-rays and two opinions, it was determined that the unfortunate Megan needed surgery to remove the unusual stomach contents. Luckily, Megan survived it all and was returned home, shaken but undaunted, to Lynn.

Along this line it is well to remind everyone that dogs cannot handle chocolate very well. It produces tachycardia (a fast heartbeat) and also acts as a diuretic. Many dogs are allergic to it. The culprit ingredient is theobromine, which comprises a much higher percent of unsweetened baker's chocolate than of milk chocolate. Unsweetened chocolate has 450 mg per ounce; the corresponding amount in milk chocolate is 44 mg per ounce. If your dog has consumed large amounts of chocolate on the sly (as Mugwump did when she stole the Pepperidge Farm chocolate fudge cake and ate the whole thing), it is wise to get the Basset to the vet immediately. Mugwump spent the night being dosed with ipecac and vomiting voluminously all over the veterinary clinic, but returned unscathed and unrepentant. In fact, the first thing she did upon returning home was to stretch up to the counter to see if any cake was left.

Kelly O'Brien's dog, Grace, managed to combine two no-nos in one: chocolate covered espresso beans! Grace also spent some time in the clinic, ingesting activated charcoal after ingesting hydrogen peroxide to make her vomit.

Annette Green offers this:

> Regarding strange items that have passed with no apparent injury or pain, I have one to add to the list. I used to own a plastic water gun that I used on our cat, Kramer Lestat, when he was somewhere he should not have been. Anyway, our foster dog, Kip, likes to drink water from the gun. Once he saw me use the gun on Kramer and that Kramer did not like it, so he decided to remedy the situation. While I wasn't looking, he simply ate most of the gun. It passed completely without any problems.

I'm sure that Kramer Lestat was very grateful.

One item marketed for dog chews is best unbought, at least in my opinion: white rawhide chews. Some dogs are allergic to the preservative these contain (propylene glycol). The rawhide can swell up in your dog's tummy and cause all kinds of problems. Best to avoid these treats.

In this business, I get a lot of mail from dogs. Now Bassets as a group make lousy correspondents, not being able to spell or type very well, but with a little cleaning up, some of their tales are fairly presentable, even if the dogs are not. Here are two examples. The first letter is from Ms. Molly Dog, companion of Bill James:

> Ms. Molly Dog online—Just wanted to tell you about the lost treasure we discovered in the backyard today. Every day, The Bearded One (TBO) and Mrs. TBO put valuable Basset treasures into a big green box with wheels on it. The box is so tall that even I can't see exactly what is in it, but the smells are too rich to describe. Every few meals (which is how we Bassets measure time), TBO wheels the box out through the gate, and a big, noisy, smoky truck beast eats the treasures. ClioPatra, Bosley, and I bark at it and it goes away.

> Today the three of us decided to knock the treasure box over. It was almost full! Why does TBO feed all that good stuff to the beast every few meals? There was cantaloupe peel, a big package of bread that was only green around the edges, lots of neat paper stuff to make Basset confetti, an empty milk carton, and some yucky stuff that just begged to be rolled in.

> We ate, chewed, nibbled, feasted, lunched, dined, licked, slurped, and noshed until we had to take naps. Afterwards, not wanting to leave a pile of stuff for TBO to clean up, we cleverly scattered leftovers throughout the backyard so it wouldn't look too obvious. Our efforts were unappreciated. TBO got rude, chased us with the rake, and ended up cleaning the last of the yard by lamplight. Then he fastened tops on all three green treasure chests so we can't get into them even if Clio does knock them over. If TBO is really so smart, why does he feed all this good stuff to that smelly truck every week?

Good question.

This is another, from Ashley B. Hound, owned by Karen Clemente:

Hi! Last week we had a house full of people who came to visit my new brother, Jason, and give him all these new gifts. Naturally I did not like this. I should have all the gifts and all the attention. They decided to order pizza for dinner—my favorite, next to Doritos, which were also present. First, to make everyone look at me, I ate a whole bowl of Doritos and was standing on the kitchen table when Mom found me with my head in the bowl and ears full of cheese. YUM!! Mom was not amused, but everyone else was. When the pizza came and everyone was sitting around the table laughing at Jason as he tried to stuff a whole piece of pizza into his mouth, I figured I could go him one better. I very cleverly and sneakily crept up to the second pizza without anyone noticing, got it out of the box, and ran off with it. By the time Mom was ready to serve it, she discovered it was missing. I was down the hall,

When Eva and Bill Wickemeier's Basset, Baby Nugs, isn't sunbathing, he and his family are enjoying a food fight.

working on the last two pieces in the box. I had sauce, cheese, and dough all over me! My white fur was orange, my paws were full of cheese, and my belly was covered in sauce! Boy, did I have fun!

My own precious Mugwump is fond of yanking things off the counter—Bassets are amazingly long dogs when standing upright. This habit is called "counter cruising," by the way. The other day she pulled an entire bowl of spaghetti sauce upside down on her head. The other dogs licked it off her. Now that was an accident, but Eva Wickemeier writes:

My husband feeds the Bassets leftover spaghetti by throwing it on their backs. They eat it off each other. This is big fun at our house.

Who says basseteers don't know how to live it up?

Dennis Owen had a pair of Bassets who, working together, managed to steal 11 boxes of Girl Scout cookies before he caught the pair running through the doggie door with a box each.

Amy Zaremski adapted the "Twelve Days of Christmas" song to enumerate her Basset's exploits. The quantities aren't quite accurate, but Amy guarantees that Raleigh has eaten at least one of everything on the list:

12 Christmas cards	6 pencils snapping
11 plastic milk jugs	5 pig ears
10 chips and salsa	4 pairs of socks
9 loaves of bread	3 French rolls
8 petunias blooming	2 expensive shoes
7 Milk Bones crunching	1 hole in the kitchen floor

My favorite correspondence along this line, however, has to come from Carrie Schadle, who wrote calmly:

Romeo is pretty much too lazy to eat anything unless it is (or used to be) food, but when he was a puppy he ate a whole wicker basket and some really big fireworks my mother had sent me.

I couldn't top this and asked Carrie for a follow-up. She wrote:

> *When Romeo ate the fireworks I was, of course, very concerned and opened the Yellow Pages to find an emergency vet. When I found one and told her that my dog had just eaten fireworks, she paused for a second, then asked: "What kind of dog is he?" When I told her he was a Basset, she said, "Oh . . ." in a very knowing way and asked me to hold while she went to look it up. For some reason, she had never heard of a dog eating fireworks before. While I was on hold, Romeo threw up the fireworks on my bed, looking as perky as ever.*

Ah, those Bassets. . . .

It's a well-known fact, however, that thrown up fireworks do not work as well as new ones. This may have been Romeo's intention all along. Dogs hate fireworks.

Well, is there anything a Basset can't eat?

Yes! Poisonous plants, for one thing. These include columbine (*Aquilegia vulgaris*), star-of-Bethlehem (*Ornithogalum umbellatum*), yew (*Taxus baccata*), lupine (*Lupinus*), clematis, lily of the valley (*Convallaria majalis*), boxwood (*Buxus sempervirens*), jimsonweed (*Datura stramonium*), hemlock (*Conium maculatum*), daffodils, mayapple (*Podophyllum peltatum*), monkshood (*Aconitum uncinatum*), and ivy (*Hedera*).

Your Basset probably won't be tempted to eat most of these things, although considering the diet list (see above), I wouldn't be too sure. Still, it's wise to be prudent. I've seen the result of cattle inadvertently poisoned with yew, and it was not a pretty sight (imagine about 25 head of cattle lying dead in a pasture—the result of a kindly but ill-informed neighbor throwing the cuttings of his ornamental yew hedge into the neighboring field because he thought the cows might like them. Unfortunately, they did.) It's a pretty safe bet that most things that can kill a cow can likewise kill a Basset Hound.

A few things exist that, although not poisonous, are distasteful—at least to some Bassets. This list, culled from Basset owners around the country, includes:

Bananas	Grapes (several nominations)
Black jelly beans	Green beans
Broccoli and cauliflower (unless smothered in cheese sauce)	Green peppers
	Lettuce (several nominations)
	Lobster
Clams	Mushrooms
Dill pickles	Olives (several nominations)
Dog breath mints (even when disguised as lumps of peanut butter)	Onions
	Popcorn (except caramel)
	Potato chips
Dog food	Shrimp (several nominations)
Eggs	Walnuts

Judith Schmidt says her Shelby "turns her nose up at the bland IAMS treats that the neighbor keeps trying to give her. She hides them in her mouth and delicately spits them out when her back is turned away from him." Bassets never like to hurt people's feelings, which is why I'm convinced that they humor us when we play the "Let's see if he'll eat **this,**" game.

Noah Stewart's Buster will eat broken fluorescent light tubes, but not peas. He says:

> I gave him some leftover stew once, with peas in it. When I returned to his dish some time later, I found all the peas neatly racked in the bottom. That explained the "ptoo" sounds I kept hearing.

Teresa Murphy's Basset, Skittles, won't eat mushrooms, even, Teresa says, when they're on pizza—which Skittles loves!

How about food allergies?

Thumbing through *Small Animal Dermatology* (Robert Kirk and George Muller, 1995; W. B. Saunders), a wildly fun bedtime read, by the way, I discovered a list of "dietary items that have caused food hypersensitivity in dogs." The list included the following, in alphabetical order: artificial food additives, beef, canned foods, chicken, corn, cow's milk, dairy products, dog biscuits, dog food, eggs, fish, food preservatives, horse meat, kidney beans, lamb and mutton, oatmeal, pasta, pork, potatoes, rabbit, rice and rice flour, soy, turkey, and wheat. Notice there is nothing on the list about disposable razors, underwear, lightbulbs, and firecrackers.

Dogs can even be allergic to plastic, especially the kind of plastic that some dog food dishes are made from. By using plastic plates, your dog may develop strange bumps on his chin. If this is the case, try stainless steel dishes. Plastic dishes have the added disadvantage that, over time, they are impossible to get really clean—tiny particles of food and their accompanying bacteria can become permanent residents of the minuscule dents.

Speaking of dishes, you can purchase special designed-for-Bassets water and food dishes—deeper than they are wide. These work pretty well for keeping your hound's precious ears out of his food or water. I recommend them.

EIGHT

Caring for Your Basset

My Basset smells. What can I do about it?

A fact of life about Basset Hounds is B.O. (Basset Odor), a heady aroma redolent of musty socks and an unkempt compost heap. Why **do** Bassets (and other hounds) smell so . . . so awful? No one really knows, but I think it has something to do with pack identification. Hounds are much more pack-oriented than are other dog types; perhaps the smell contributes to the camaraderie. (This is all just a guess on my part, though.)

GRACIE   **Pam Posey-Tanzey**

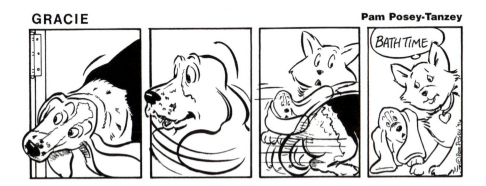

The doggy odor so disliked by some and so adored by others is caused by apocrine sweat glands, which our houndy pals have in abundance all over their fat little bodies. Apocrine sweat glands don't operate the way the ones in your armpits do, though; they're completely useless for controlling temperature. Their primary function seems to be to make the owner wrinkle her nose and say, "Ick! It's time this animal had a bath!" The bad smell comes from the nasty bacteria that help break down the secretions from the gland. In order to sweat properly, Bassets need to rely on the eccrine sweat glands in their paw pads, which tend to give off an odor redolent of stale popcorn. These glands also double as moisture providers—our hounds need to keep their pads soft and resilient. When serious sweating is required—as in the well-named dog days of August—dogs pant, which is nothing more than sweating through their tongues.

GRACIE

Pam Posey-Tanzey

My own solution to the odor problem is baths—and lots of 'em. I'm a bath freak, as far as my Bassets go. Like many people, I grew up hearing and reading that baths were bad for dogs, that they took away their "natural oils" and dried out their skin. In other words, I grew up with a lot of smelly, shedding, flea-ridden, scabby animals of various breeds. Now, however, I bathe my dogs at least twice a week, using a mild human shampoo. It is true that dog skin and human skin have different pH values, but too much should not be made of this. No research indicates that using a shampoo designed for people hurts a dog's skin in any way. Just be sure to rinse your dog thoroughly—it should take at least twice as long to rinse him as it did to soap him up.

The results have been spectacular: soft shiny coats and no skin problems. The shed hair goes mostly into the bathtub rather than onto the couch. Bassets, by the way, shed year-round, all year, every day, no relief, and no letup. But baths help. They really, really do. The best result of frequent baths, however, is: NO HOUND SMELL. Flea and tick problems are reduced to a minimum without the use of harsh chemicals. And because of the careful going over they get at bathtime, minor nicks or other problems are quickly detected.

Now that I think about it, it seems like a natural solution. In medieval times, for instance, when we human beings weren't too particular about bathing ourselves, one of our closest companions was not our faithful Hound, but *Pulex irritans*, the human flea, which indeed has played such a fascinating role in our history. Most notably, it can host *Yersina pestis*, the bacterial strain that causes the Black Death. Well, that's another story.

I know that frequent bathing is not a solution for everyone—in fact, I've even heard of one person who actually likes hound smell—but it's something to consider. My dogs always get a treat afterward, and while they are not enamored with the idea of baths, they will submit to them without too much complaining. (They do insist on that treat afterward, though.)

If you still aren't sold on the twice-a-week bath idea, you can try a lamb and rice dry food diet. I'm told that it helps.

Help! My Basset was skunked!

Forget the tomato juice. It doesn't work. What does work is Massangil Douche powder, used, of course, on the outside of the dog. You'll have to use a lot of it, thereby necessitating several trips to the grocery store. Obviously you can't get it all in one trip. Too many strange looks. If, as I suspect, (especially if you're a man), you are too much of a sissy to buy douche powder in suitable quantities, you may need to resort to a commercial product like Skunk Kleen. The problem with stuff like this is that your dog will be skunked at 2 am when no pet stores are open. Don't be surprised. Skunks are nocturnal animals, as it happens.

Another thing that seems to work is Lestoil. If you follow a Lestoil bath with a mild shampoo and rinse, you shouldn't have any problems. Or at least no more than you might expect. Besides, skunk smells don't last forever, even though it may seem like it. Why in a month or two, you might not even notice it.

What do I do about gummy armpits?

If you have gummy armpits, try taking a bath. If your Basset has the same problem, wash the area gently and rinse it well. Some people recommend a dandruff shampoo, and others have had tremendous luck with Pert Plus. Follow up with Gold Bond powder. It works wonders. For some reason, Basset Hounds seem prone to this condition. No one knows why.

Do I really need to brush my Basset's teeth?

Of course. It's not a big deal. My dogs actually like it and line up for the toothbrush. Of course, you will use a made-for-dogs kind of toothpaste, not Colgate. You can buy a little made-for-doggy-teeth toothbrush, or you can just use your finger, which I would recommend (at least in the beginning). The paste is chicken or beef flavored, so first let your greedy hound lick it from your finger, so he will get used to the idea. Then rub your finger gently around the outside of his teeth, a little at a time. The outside is much easier to reach than the inside, which is lucky, since that's where all the crud accumulates anyway.

How should I groom my Basset?

Try a hound mitt! This device slips over your hand like a glove. Brushing your Basset's coat in firm, circular strokes will improve his circulation, get rid of dead, loose hair (at least some of it—don't worry, there's always more), and provide him with a sense of being loved and cared for. A hound mitt is really all you need, although the kind people at the pet supply store will attempt to convince you otherwise. You may wish to invest in a flea comb also, which will help you spot any of the little parasites.

Should I buy my Basset a toy?

Sure, go ahead. But there's no guarantee that he'll play with it, although you might. As a group, hounds are less playful than other breeds. They're serious dogs, with important things to think about, like food. Most Bassets appreciate squeaky toys, but don't leave them around all the time or the hound will quickly become bored.

Bassets aren't thrilled with the game of fetch either. They think if you want to throw things around like that, you can jolly well go and get them yourself, without bothering His Majesty.

I have never seen a Basset yet that has the remotest interest in a hard rubber bone.

If you want to play with your dog, get out the leash and walk him. That's what he likes best.

Second choice: Get him another Basset Hound.

Should I get my Basset neutered?

Yes. Please. In this country, over 20,000,000 pets are put to death annually by shelters. Untold others die in far more brutal ways. Contrary to common belief, many of these pathetic creatures are not strays or mongrels. They are purebred dogs and cats whose owners have grown tired of them. Many people purchase a pet because their children want one (and then ignore it), or because it's faddish to own a certain kind of dog or cat. We don't need any more kittens or puppies in the world right this minute. We do need to find homes for the ones we now have. The only exception to this, I feel, is a knowledgeable, committed breeder who knows what she or he is doing and who is NOT trying to make a living from breeding dogs. Ask yourself the following questions:

1. Is your Basset registered? (If not, **get your dog neutered.**)

2. Does your Basset's bloodline have at least **four** Champions in the last three generations, in conformation, obedience, field trials, or tracking? (If not, **get your dog neutered.** Championships any further back than three generations are worthless.)

3. Do you want to breed your dog so your kids can experience the sacred mystery of birth? (If so, **get your dog neutered.** Plenty of good videos are available. They're cheaper and a lot less messy.)

4. Are you under the illusion that breeding your dog is a quick way to make a few bucks? (If so, **get your dog neutered.** Even if this were true, it would be scandalous for you to use your friend in such a way. And, it's not true. It may in fact cost you money, especially if you are conscientious about medical care. The only people who make a profit from breeding dogs run what are called "puppy mills." Puppy mills are dog versions of concentration camps.)

5. Do you think it's "healthy" for a dog to have a litter of puppies? It's not. Unspayed female dogs are subject to a host of illnesses, especially mammary cancer, from which their spayed sisters are virtually free. Unspayed females who have had puppies are at even greater risk. Pregnancies are potentially life threatening for any species and should be risked only for sound reasons. Allowing your dog to

become pregnant is not doing her a favor. Unless you are willing to risk increases in mammary cancer, in addition to the risks of whelping, **get your dog neutered.** Likewise, unneutered male dogs run the risk of developing testicular cancer.

6. Is your dog completely free of all genetic disorders? (If your answer is no or you're not sure, **get your dog neutered.** Passing on your dog's problems to future generations is immoral.)

7. Is your Basset an outstanding example of the breed? (If not, **get your dog neutered.** Only show quality dogs should be bred. Do not even think about breeding your dog if she deviates from the breed standard.)

8. Do you want to breed your dog because puppies are cute and you want some around for a few weeks? (Think again. If this is your primary reason for breeding, check into a mental health clinic and **get your dog neutered.**) According to breeder Mary Lou Chipman, of Wagtail Bassets in Fredericksburg, Virginia, Basset puppies should be kept home for 12 weeks, during which period they will have most of their puppy shots. (Are you prepared to give those yourself?) Most people want to get a puppy at eight weeks, when they're the "cutest," but this is much too early. Bassets need another month to be properly socialized. That's 12 weeks of cleaning up urine, feces, vomit, destroyed shoes, and shredded clothes and paper. During those 12 weeks, you need to look out for your puppies constantly, for fear they'll fall ill or hurt themselves. Basset puppies become mobile after four or five weeks and will ransack your house. This does not mean, however, that they are old enough to leave their mother.

9. Are you competent to handle any medical emergencies that arise with puppies? (If not, **get your dog neutered.**)

11. Are you willing to risk the death of your mother dog? Your dog can die from giving birth. Are you willing to take that responsibility? (If not, **get your dog neutered.** If so, ask yourself why.)

12. Are you willing to do elaborate check-ups on people who may (and believe me, the operative word is "may") want to buy a puppy? (If not, **get your dog neutered.**) Will you do a house-check? What

evidence do you have that the new owners will not irresponsibly breed your puppies? How many future generations are you willing to add to the death toll?

13. Are you actively involved in showing or working your dog? (If not, **get your dog neutered.**)

14. Are you an expert on Basset Hounds, their history, their breed standard, and their various lines? Are you familiar with the basics of genetics? Is your primary reason for breeding the improvement of the breed? Harry Chipman is very blunt about this. He and Mary Lou breed only when they have something they feel will improve their line or Bassets in general. He says, "What will result from this breeding that will improve the breed?" (If you can't answer that question, **get your dog neutered.**)

Please, act responsibly and with love. Neuter your pet.

Mary Lou and Harry Chipman only breed their Bassets when they believe they can improve their line or the breed. The outcome of careful breeding is a fine Basset, like Mischief Maker.

Do I really need to trim my Basset's nails?

Yes, indeed. In fact, nail trimming is probably **more** important for Bassets than for almost any other breed. Basset feet tend to splay under the best of conditions, and long nails make this tendency even worse, thus upsetting the dog's natural (or in the case of Bassets, **unnatural**) balance. To make things more difficult, many Bassets have toenails like two by fours, and many Bassets hate the nail-trimming procedure so much they'll make you wish you were dead rather than undertake it.

Fortunately, there is an answer! Try **grinding** your precious puppy's nails! Using a Dremel nail grinder has taken the heartbreak out of trimming around here. Although it took two weeks of everyday desensitizing to get our dogs used to the noise and vibration, they are now so comfortable with the grinding procedure that they literally lie down and wave their paws in the air! It takes only one person—not three the way it used to. The grinder works quickly—but slowly enough so that you will not cause bleeding—even on those tricky black nails where the quick is invisible. In case you do make an error in trimming, keep a supply of styptic powder on hand to stop the bleeding.

Your dog should **not** bleed when you clip his nails any more than you should. Sometimes show dogs are shown with unnaturally short nails, under some mistaken impression that it looks good. The nails should come just short of the floor and not click when the Basset walks on tile, but they shouldn't be any shorter. The dog needs a proper nail length for running; it helps maintain his grip and balance.

Fleas, ticks, and flies, oh my!

Fleas love Basset Hounds, but as mentioned above, you can really cut down on their presence with frequent bathing. In addition, you should vacuum your house, including your furniture, and launder your dog's bedding often—a least once a week.

Flea collars are of minimal use, dipping is hard on your dog's system, and many new anti-flea techniques are expensive or of doubtful efficacy. One of the best is Frontline, a topical, inexpensive treatment for your dog's skin that is low in side effects and high in effectiveness. As I said before, frequent bathing works simple wonders.

Ticks are another matter. Ticks laugh at baths. They laugh at tick collars, too. You must simply check your dog every day during tick season, especially in the wet springtime, and pluck the ghastly creatures out. **Do not use your bare fingers.** A tiny opening around your nails might be all that's needed for you to acquire Rocky Mountain fever, Lyme disease, or a number of other nasty ailments. Dogs can be vaccinated against Lyme disease, but you can't, at least not yet. Once the nasty tick is in your gloved or tissued hand, toss the critter in the toilet and flush.

We all know about fleas and ticks, so let's say a word about **flies.** There's a terrible little beastie up and about these days called **cuterebra.** Only there's nothing cute about these critters. They hang around your yard's grass as little eggs, then as larvae, just waiting for your innocent Basset to hobble by. They can infest your pet just underneath the skin, where they can develop into a monstrous maggot an inch long! (All you might see is a lump.) This infestation occurs most commonly in the late summer and fall, so be on the lookout. The whole notion is so disgusting I can hardly stand to write about it.

How hard it is to travel with a Basset?

Oh, it's a great deal of fun. Take this story from Patty Nordstrom, told from the point of view of her delightful Smuckers:

> *I just spent a weekend at Grandma's house. What fun! It is a three and a half hour trip, and I like to cry and whine until we get on the interstate. Even though Dad talks to me while Mom is driving, I just do not like those twisty mountain roads. Once on the interstate, we stop at the rest area. Mom takes me out and we widdle and get a drink of water. Then Mom and Dad disappear into a building for a while—it seems like forever. But guess what I find while they are gone—CHOCOLATE Cake! Dad opens the car door and says, "Smuckers is eating the cake!"*
>
> *Mom says, "No way can she get into that cake carrier." WRONG! I didn't get much, but what I got was great. Dad thinks all this is pretty funny, but Mom is not happy. She doesn't speak to me or Dad for the next 100 miles.*
>
> *We get to Grandma's house and I want to play, but everyone else wants to go to bed. I run around the house: aroooo, arooo. I can't sleep in the bed with Mom and Dad, since it's only a double and I weigh 65 pounds. Mom sleeps on the couch with me.*

Sometimes domestic travel can present a problem. My red Basset, Ruby, for example, is prone to car sickness. I discovered this interesting fact one day soon after I got her. I had decided to take her along with me to school to show her off to my students and was driving merrily along, when she got a terrible case of nausea and threw up all over the gear shift.

Beth Fuller had a similar experience:

> *When Rosebud was a puppy, I was taking her and Daisy for a weekend at my mother's house—about a two-hour drive. Before we got a mile away from home, Rosebud threw up in my purse! No kidding, every bit of it went right into my open purse!*

Later, on a different trip, Daisy threw up on Beth's car phone. And she wonders why no one wants to go anywhere with her.

Beth Fuller's Basset, Rosebud (pictured here between her friends, Lily and Daisy), had a hard time adjusting to car rides.

The real key to successful Basset travel is to take your dog with you everywhere you can. The more the Basset becomes used to travel, the less of a big deal it will be and the more comfortable for all concerned. If the only times you take your dog into a car are for a run in the meadows or to go to the vet's, your poor pet will hover constantly in an approach-avoidance mode that can make him difficult to deal with. Try taking your pet with you when you drive to the bank, the dry cleaner's, and the library. (Our library welcomes dogs—unofficially, of course.) The rides will be a welcome change of pace for him, and he will learn that not every car trip will result in a life-changing experience. When you arrive at your destination, take him out of the car and encourage him to meet people. (Of course, you are sure that your Basset will behave in a reasonable way on such occasions.) The more he accompanies you, the better behaved he will become and a greater pleasure he will be to bring along on every trip.

Never under any circumstances allow your dog to travel free in the back of a pickup truck! One good jounce could pitch your friend out of the truck and onto the highway. Nor is it sufficient to attach him by his collar;

it's an invitation to having his neck broken. It is by far the best plan to have him securely crated so he won't be exposed to road debris, errant rocks, and undue jostling.

In general, if you must go on a long trip, feed your Basset lightly before setting out, but not **just before**. Give him a chance to use the facilities, so to speak, before you leave. Keep your Basset snug in a seat belt, and stop every few hours for a walk and water. Most dogs will soon go to sleep; on our way to the Great Michigan Basset Waddle, Ruby and Mugwump slept steadily for five or six hours. It's a good idea, by the way, to bring along your own water—just in case. Some dogs, especially puppies, are susceptible to diarrhea when exposed to different water. Canine diarrhea is not pleasant to deal with at any time, and diarrhea that strikes when you're traveling along the interstate with your Basset is fairly close to intolerable. Take no chances. On the same note, be sure to bring paper towels. Remember: drool, urine, diarrhea, and vomit. Bring a whole roll.

Some states require current rabies vaccination certificates for dogs being shipped. It's a good idea to always have one in the car when traveling, just in case. It won't hurt anything.

I have to travel overseas. Can I take my Basset?

Maybe. My favorite travel story comes from Alvaro Aguilar, a correspondent from Panama, whose dog Chandler faced a 40-day quarantine. "When everything but hope was lost," he explained, "the people at the Panama Health Ministry told me that I should write an appeal to the Minister explaining why 40 days of quarantine would harm my precious Chandler. I did just that and enclosed a picture of Chandler in a typically Basset-like pose (sad look, crooked legs). Needless to say, in one day (instead of the one week expected), the Minister authorized a residential quarantine plan that allowed twice daily visits with Chandler!"

Alvaro had some other great tips for international travelers: Always check quarantine requirements at the destination with a vet in that location (the U.S. Embassy was clueless about the situation in Panama). Get a health certificate with a list of all vaccinations, especially rabies, and have it authenticated at the consulate of the country of destination. No authentication gives you a worthless piece of paper. Reserve a pressurized compartment for the dog in advance. Have the dog travel in a sturdy kennel (see below), with toys, two cups of water, and the address of the consignee written with a marker on the container (not just a label that may fall off). Avoid traveling on Fridays because the quarantine authority at the destination may be out for the weekend, and if the dog arrives in the late afternoon, he may spend a very uncomfortable weekend in a cage.

Your dog must travel in a container that complies with the guidelines set down by the International Air Transport Association. This means a strong frame, one end of which must be "open" so the animal can breathe. The opposite end of the container must also be well ventilated with holes or slots (which must be smaller than the dog's nose). The door must be hinged or sliding and "very secure." The container should be large enough for the animal to stand, turn, and lie down. A "Live Animal" label must be affixed to the top, as well as a "This Way Up" sign. Make sure the dog's name, as well as your own name and address, is attached. Put a familiar toy or comfort item in with your dog.

Puppies younger than eight weeks should not be shipped, nor should females in heat or nursing.

"Free for dinner?"

Panama seems to be a trial for Bassets and their owners, but the clever Basset owner can circumvent many obstacles. Take this other Panama tale, offered by Randy Noller:

While in quarantine, Chester wouldn't eat—VERY rare for Chester. He was losing weight fast, and the only thing I could get him to eat was a cheeseburger from the Burger King on Fort Clayton. Even then, he'd only eat it from my hand. If I laid it down, he'd walk away. In 10 days he lost 12 pounds.

Finally we got him out of jail and into another nicer jail (really a kennel) next to the guest house I was staying in. The guest house, however, didn't allow pets, and I couldn't stand the way poor Chester was being treated. One day I took my large black duffel bag into the kennel. I opened it up, laid it on the floor, and explained to Chester that he had to ride in it so that we wouldn't get caught and thrown out. I swear he understood because he walked into the bag, sat down, and looked up at me as if he was asking "What now?"

After that I'd give him a ride into my room each evening and out again in the morning. He slept with me every night and never made a sound in my room. The Cuna Indian guys who clean the guest house had it figured out after the first four or five days. They would grin and point to the bag; I would put my finger to my lips and smile, and they would say "Si, no problemo!" Chester lived with me in the guest house for almost a month before we got a house. Chester and I have become very close; I tell everyone he is my son. I think Chester and I both believe it.

When you can't take him along

Pam Posey-Tanzey

This is an agonizing decision for the devoted Basseteer. We all want to take our beloved hounds wherever we go, but there are still times when it is impossible, or at least inappropriate. Believe it or not, there are still some benighted hotels that won't accept dogs—even Bassets. Therefore we are sometimes forced to consider alternate care for our dogs. We worry about everything: "Will my Basset be able to cope? Will I? Will he get sick? Will I?" And so on. Ronald Saunders writes:

> Maggie knows when I am packing things up for a big trip . . . and she refuses to get into the car! But the people at the kennel are great, and they say that she adjusts really well when I leave. They actually have more problems with the owners and their long, teary good-byes.

Although your Basset may howl mournfully, and even roll over and play dead when you take him to be boarded, chances are that the minute you leave, he will be playing happily. Steel yourself. You'll miss him more than he'll miss you.

On the other side are Bassets like the one belonging to Doug Rosen:

> I bet he thinks it's a vacation. I travel a lot for business and he gets boarded for a few days every month. He goes off tail wagging. He is always very excited to see me again, but he never gets upset when going back to the vet's.

For some, even the everyday going-to-work routine is agonizing. It doesn't have to be. Chances are, if you don't make a big deal of it, neither will your Basset. Do not behave as if it were the end of the world; tears, screams, and heartfelt throbs are quite unnecessary. Give your pet a curt but friendly nod, quick pat on the head, and "Bye-bye, Fred. See ya around five." Hand him a dog biscuit as you leave, and **don't look back.** If you do, you may become—like Orpheus or Lot's wife—lost forever. On your return, explain to your Basset that: (a) you were kidnapped by pirates and held for ransom until that very moment or (b) you were out slaving for his dog food and vet bills. This may make you feel better, even as you're given the most frozen of stares (sometimes interspersed with wild face-licking) from your deeply injured Basset friend.

Another excellent solution for many are the services of an experienced pet sitter. There are many agencies who do this; some even give shots, and visits can be scheduled as your budget permits, even as many as four a day. Of course, if you can con your mother into doing this chore, it's even better. She might clean your oven, too. The great advantage of this approach is that your Bassets will be in their own dear home. You can call them on the phone and speak sweetly to them.

When you do return home, however, be prepared for the silent treatment. Bassets do not easily forgive.

NINE

Under the Weather: The Beast Is Indisposed

Like all sentient creatures (with the possible exception of sharks), Basset Hounds are subject to a variety of illnesses. Since this is not a medical book (and there are plenty of good ones out there), we'll just go over the most important points. As a side note, it may interest you to know that you and your Basset can share more than love and affection—humans share 65 diseases with their canine friends, more than with any other domestic animal. (Goats, believe it or not, come in second with 46, pigs with 42, 35 for horses, 32 for rats and mice, and 26 for poultry. Personally, I think it would be rather embarrassing to catch something from a chicken, but there you are.)

Actually, Bassets are quite pleasant to have around when you are ill. They are very comforting. Sue Lockhart's dog, Boss, writes:

> I have had to go into physical therapy. The woman has come down with a bad back, and I've been working very hard as a heating pad. She'd been fooling with hot water bottles, electric heating pads, etc. until I demonstrated that Bassets are the perfect size to stretch out along the length of a human back. I'm also doing some counseling. My method is to groan along with the sufferer. If she groans a bit, I groan a lot louder. It seems to work, since she ends up laughing. The woman says I've found my true calling: I was born to be a heating pad.

"Do you ever have a pulse?"

I've found out that a smallish Basset makes a perfect massager, also. Just lie on your stomach and encourage your Basset to walk on your back. Much cheaper than a chiropractor.

If your special friend should become ill, follow the first rule of first aid: Get a good vet, one who understands the special characteristics of Basset Hounds. All breeds have particular problems to which they are susceptible. Some of these may be hereditary; some are conditions to which the Basset's odd physique makes it prone. In the latter category, for example, it is good to know that finding a good site for intravenous injections may be tough in Basset Hounds. Since Basset Hounds are not a particularly common breed, this may come as a surprise to your vet.

The taint of blood: inherited problems

Thankfully, hereditary diseases are uncommon among Bassets. There are three, however, that I would like to consider briefly. These are: luxating patella (slipped kneecap), glaucoma, and ectropion. Luxating patella is an ailment of the hind leg and can be surgically repaired. Ectropion is a condition of loose eyelids, again a condition that may be surgically corrected. Glaucoma results from an increase in fluid pressure inside the eye. Pressure-reducing medication is available, which must be taken for the life of the dog. Extremely painful cases may require surgical removal of the eye. Blindness in dogs, by the way, while no joke, is not the extraordinary disability in dogs that it is in human beings. In this regard, I'd like to mention Chelsea, Melinda Brown's blind foster Basset. Chelsea had been bought as a puppy by a college student. When she came down with glaucoma, however, she became "too much of a bother." The student handed her over to her mother, who passed her along to a boarding kennel and promptly forgot about her. Eventually the dog was advertised in the paper to be given away and thus came to the attention of Basset Hound Rescue. This is where Melinda Brown stepped in. Melinda, a basseteer extraordinaire, took the year-old-plus Chelsea home as a foster dog, undaunted by the prospect of a blind Basset. Chelsea had other problems, too, she was allergic to herself! When placed on high dosages of prednisone, however, the rawness and swelling resulting from her constantly licking herself disappeared.

In spite of her handicap, Chelsea became an amazingly trainable dog. Since she was told that Chelsea liked the security of a crate, Melinda had one set up in the family room. Soon Chelsea learned where the water bowls were and where the door to go out was located. Since exiting Melinda's house requires negotiating stairs, Melinda was there to help. As she writes:

> *For every step, I'd say, "Step down," and when she got to the last step, I'd say, "Last one." It didn't take her long to get the count of the stairs, and soon she was doing pretty well without our help. Within a week, Chelsea was moving around our house with ease. I was amazed at how well adjusted she was and how she was not at all afraid of attempting new things.*

> *When the weather began to turn fine and we started to get the dogs out for more walks, Chelsea really began to blossom. One of her most looked-for treats was the morning walk. Contrary to what you might imagine, she walks out boldly, seemingly unconcerned that she can't see. She sticks to the sidewalk, and if she veers to the left or right, she corrects herself when she hits the grass edges. In fact, going down the sidewalk, she kind of looks like the ball in a bumper pool game, bouncing from one side to the other.*

> *I decided early in March that Chelsea had what it takes to pass the Canine Good Citizen test and resolved to get it for her.*

And got it she did. Chelsea passed the test with flying colors and is now an official Canine Good Citizen.

The bittersweet ending to Chelsea's story is this: She has been permanently adopted by a family from South Carolina, who was looking for a quiet companion to their own Basset, an invalid with an enlarged heart. Melinda writes:

> *My last sight of her was the same as the first: sitting quietly in the car seat, staring into space with those enlarged, opaque eyes. But this is the last time she'll have to adjust to a new home.*

Melinda was now free to take on her next foster dog challenge.

Other common problems in Bassets

Other problems, not always hereditary, which show up relatively frequently in Basset Hounds include the following:

1. **Panosteitis:** This is a condition affecting the long bones of Basset Hounds and other large breeds of dogs. Panosteitis, also called wandering lameness, is not a primary bone disease. The cause of the disease is unknown, but it does not appear to result from trauma.

   Panosteitis is more common in males than in females and usually appears between 5 and 12 months of age, although it has been reported as early as 2 months and as late as 5 years. When it occurs in females, it is usually associated with the dog's first heat, or estrus. Affected animals have acute lameness, which may be severe. The lameness is often intermittent and may be present in more than one limb. The disease usually begins in the front limbs and commonly resolves in one location before shifting to another. Two to three week intervals may be present between episodes of lameness. Usually, one leg bone is affected at a time, and the disease rarely reoccurs in a previously affected bone. The interval between lameness episodes usually increases as the dog matures. Fever, lethargy, and loss of appetite may be observed in conjunction with panosteitis.

   Diagnosis of panosteitis involves discomfort on deep palpation and confirmation by X-ray examination. Standard treatment includes supportive care and analgesics to relieve discomfort. Dogs suffering from this condition usually recover completely, although slowly, and further complications are rare.

   In general, it is **not** a good idea to let your Basset Hound jump. They are not very good at it anyway, as a rule, and usually only embarrass themselves. It is also very bad for their legs and back.

2. **Allergies:** As Gretchen Laffert says:

   Allergies are sometimes very difficult to treat. Last summer, Zach picked up a few fleas when we were on vacation. The poor little boy suffered for four months just from the flea bites. I tried everything from benadryl to prednisone, and nothing really worked. I ended up bathing him often and

using vet wrap and socks on his four feet. . . . I also used, and I know
this sounds weird, Murphy's Oil Soap diluted 1:2 with water and bathed
him often—not anywhere near his eyes, of course. I also started giving
him OFA Fatty Acids (with no preservatives) as a supplement, and the
itch finally went away.

Gretchen also recommends using wet black tea bags for hot spots, letting the tea bag sit there for about 10 minutes until the urge to scratch or bite at the hot spot is gone.

3. **Bloat:** Bloat is the common name for gastric contortion, unfortunately common in deep-chested dogs. It is an extremely dangerous condition and can be fatal if not caught in time. Unfortunately, "caught in time" may mean 15 minutes. First aid is ineffective. The dog's stomach will appear swollen, and the animal will hunch over in pain. Get the dog to a vet immediately. Basset-L's beloved Katsie, rescued from a puppy mill, died of bloat at age 11, and Jane Holeywell's Freckles almost died of it as well. Smaller, more frequent feedings, raising the dog's water dish, and reducing stress may help prevent bloat.

4. **Skin problems:** The most common skin problem you may have to deal with in the Basset is primary seborrhea, which is probably an inherited disorder. First signs occur early in life, and as with so much else in this universe, they get worse with increasing age. Canine primary seborrhea comes in two basic forms: dry and greasy. Bassets tend to be afflicted with the greasy kind. It can spread over the whole body, but it tends to be concentrated in various body folds, particularly the face and neck. The dog also smells bad. The condition can develop into secondary bacterial infections and pruritus.

Unfortunately, there is no cure for this disorder. But it can be managed with appropriate antibiotics and a cleanliness regimen that should include frequent bathing (two or three times a week) with the mildest effective shampoo. Medicated shampoos containing sulfur and salicylic acid, or mild tar products, may prove useful. You may want to alternate stronger medicated shampoos with mild unmedicated ones.

5. **Blocked anal glands:** This is an unpleasant condition that many Bassets suffer. Sometimes blocked anal glands can even become infected, in which case antibiotics may have to be directly injected into them. Surgery is a possibility, but it should be a last resort only. Mary Lou Chipman writes:

> *If the problem is just that your dog's anal glands fill up often, learn how to express them yourself. It's smelly but not difficult. Clean them out once or twice a week, and the problem should be taken care of. It helps if you have a nice smelling doggie spray to refresh the rear end when you clean them.*

Gretchen Laffert adds:

> *Right on the money, Mary Lou! The dog may also just need a change of diet. Some vets are too quick to touch the knife.*

On the other hand, Beth Fuller writes:

> *Rosebud was having problems with her anal glands, which have been destroyed with iodine injections over the past few months. They are technically still there, but are small, hard, and do not produce any more. Surgery was never mentioned to me.*

Beth feels that surgery sounds like a quicker, less painful route than the one she took.

Make sure you understand the vet's instructions, and then obey them! It makes little sense to pay out big bucks for advice and then not follow it.

6. **Disk problems:** Long dogs on short legs tend to suffer more back problems than do their more reasonably built comrades. As you probably know, the bones of the spine, called vertebrae, are small, round bones linked with ligaments and separated by pads that act as mini-shock absorbers. Bassets, unfortunately, tend to lose suppleness in the spine at a fairly early age and can suffer disk protrusion (sometimes inaccurately called a "slipped disk"). It usually hits very suddenly and is accompanied by pain, a hunched back, lameness, or the inability to move the head. Contact your vet right away.

7. **Red eyes:** This may be normal! The haw, or nictating membrane, is a third eyelid. In most breeds it's nearly invisible, but it's sometimes prominent in Basset Hounds—and often very red. The redness may get more noticeable with increasing age or disease. If you're uncertain about what is normal for your dog, consult your vet. Eyesight is too precious, even for the nose-oriented Basset, for you to waste time wondering about it. As far as Basset vision is concerned: They cannot see in color and don't have good stereoscopic vision, but they can see well at night (at least better than we can). They also perceive moving objects much better than stationary ones. They can't judge distances very well, which adds to their inability to gauge the width of spaces that they are trying to jump.

8. **Ear problems:** Floppy-eared dogs like Bassets tend to have ear problems. Floppy ears are a sign of domestication (no wild animal has floppy ears); as a rule, the more floppy, the more domesticated. You can see how a Basset Hound stacks up next to, say, a German Shepherd.

   Ears should be cleaned thoroughly and frequently with a mild commercial cleanser. Your vet can recommend one. If your Basset is snoozing peacefully, you can lift up his ear so that the inside is open to the circulating air. This will help dry it out.

9. **Hip dysplasia:** This is a painful condition, resulting from a developing malformation of the ball and socket joint in the hip. The head of the femoral bone rubs against the socket. Hip dysplasia is a severe and hereditary problem with many of the larger dog breeds. It is not extremely common in Bassets. If you allow your Basset to get too fat, he is, by definition, a "larger dog." Bassets gain weight very easily, especially if they are not given the exercise they require as hounds. Keep the weight off your dog—not by reducing his fat intake, but by feeding him less and exercising him often and well. Do not give him calcium supplements, which can hasten the development of hip dysplasia.

10. **Teeth problems:** Even if you brush your dog's teeth daily or weekly, as he ages, he will need routine dental care. Dogs can get gum

disease just like human beings, with the same results: loss of teeth and worse. Bacteria can enter the ravaged gumline, go straight to the pericardium, and cause heart or kidney problems! To avoid this heartache, take your Basset to your vet once a year for a clean-and-polish. Your dog will look great and feel great.

11. **Heartworm:** Heartworms are disgusting, horrible, grotesque worms who take up residence in the hearts of dogs. This is a literal, and not a figurative dwelling place. The official name of these creatures is *Dirofilaria immitis*, but by whatever name, they are deadly. They are typically found on the Atlantic and Gulf Coasts of the United States. As larvae, heartworms are carried by mosquitoes and transferred to the Basset through a mosquito bite. They burrow into the skin, find a vein, and wriggle their way into the right side of the dog's heart, where they can live for five years and grow to a length of 12 inches. Eventually they can cause cardiac failure. Although heartworm can be treated, it's by far the better plan to avoid the problem in the first place. Get your Basset on monthly heartworm medication. Even if your Basset spends most of his time indoors—it only takes one bite from an infected mosquito to kill your Basset Hound.

Tragedy . . . and a miracle!

One September afternoon, Gretchen Shelby had wonderful news for all of us:

> My young lady, Promise, has taken over motherhood of 11 orphaned pups. Devastation fell upon a breeder friend when she lost the mom during a C-section. Promise, at one and a half years old, was entering a whopping false pregnancy, so we rushed her over to see if motherhood was of interest to her. Much to our surprise, she fell hook, line, and sinker for the babies. Within 24 hours, she had dropped the hair on her belly, her milk supply was increasing, and she was lying quietly with the puppies and making them the cleanest babies on this planet.
>
> We have been monitoring her health, as she too was an orphaned puppy and, as a result, had some complications that will be lifelong. She and the 11 children are all doing well at this time.
>
> It never ceases to amaze me how wonderful our Bassets are and how there seems to be a plan or purpose in all life. Promise will likely never give birth herself, yet she adores motherhood and is getting a chance to live it and give back the gift of fostering that was given to her when her own mom died in a C-section.

At last check, Promise's own foster mom, Butter, has stepped into the breach to help out, since 11 puppies are a little much for Promise, who refused food and drink while nursing the babies. Things are going fine!

Emergency!

Although some dog owners will argue with me, I am a firm believer in collars. Always. Although it has happened that a dog has choked on a collar when the owner was absent, the following things are more likely to occur:

1. The Basset will break out of his pen/yard/crate and go wandering down the road. No collar means no easy identification. Despite the fact that tattoos and implants have become all the rage, the best chance you have of getting your Basset back is to make sure he's wearing his collar and tags. My dogs have their name and phone number stitched into the fabric of their collars. They have escaped from home and have been returned because they were easily identifiable. Do not fool yourself. Most people will shrug their shoulders and not bother if identification is not readily visible. Go ahead with more elaborate identification if you like, but never forget the collar and tags.

2. Dogs can be caught in fires, car accidents, and even floods. A dog without a collar is difficult or impossible for you or a rescue worker to catch safely. If you crate your dog for his safety, make sure a leash is clipped to the cage.

3. Dogs can attack other dogs, or be attacked by them! You need to be able to leash your pet to get him away. (I'm assuming, of course, that the Basset will be the innocent party. They always are.)

Collars, whether leather or web, should be loose enough that you can slide three fingers between the collar and the neck. Choke chains can be useful for certain situations, but avoid them on young dogs; they can damage the vertebrae in the neck. A harness is safer and probably more comfortable for the dog, and "no pull" harnesses can be useful if your Basset is stronger than you are.

A new kind of lead has been devised that acts like a horse halter; it slides over the dog's head. Your dog may resist this at first, but he will probably soon get used to it. It solves the problem of pulling completely, and even a small child can lead the largest Basset.

Restraint is the secret of happy pet ownership. Although we all love the thought of our dogs waddling wild and free through the meadows and creeks, we must not forget life's little surprises, like snakes, hornets, raging torrents, toxic waste, riptides, bigger and meaner dogs, vicious children, and cars—the ultimate enemy. If your Basset is not on a leash, you can't control him, even if he is a champion obedience dog.

Always hook your pet up with a canine seat belt when driving (assuming you are the one driving). Not only will this keep a 60-pound tub of lard off your lap, but it will also keep him safe and comfortable in the backseat. Seat belts are as important for your dog's safety as for your own or for your child's—and for the same reasons. They also prevent your dog from leaping (or waddling) out of the car whenever you stop.

Crates are good also! If you have room, a portable crate is a wonderful thing for your dog. Some can even be stacked one atop another like little efficiency apartments, in case you need to move a dozen Bassets or so around the country. You can even acquire a foldaway pup tent so to speak, which can be stashed in the smallest of cars and opened upon arrival. These were invented for show people, but I have found them of inestimable value on trips.

About medications

Next to your Basset, your vet is your best friend. Trust him or her to give you the best advice possible. This does not mean you should never seek another opinion. You should, especially in situations of serious conse-quence, either financially or medically. You would do the same for yourself. It is well known that many medications are available via mail-order cata-log for your pet. While these medications are indeed often cheaper than what you could obtain from the vet, and indeed are often used by breeders and other dog experts, it can be unwise to medicate your pet yourself. Your vet may pick up contradictions to certain medicines, which you would not be aware of. At the very least, consult with your vet before resorting to mail-order medicine.

The nice thing about getting all your medicine from your vet is that you'll feel more justified when you call him or her at 2 am, if there's an emergency. You can't call the mail-order company. It just doesn't care.

By the way, I have it on good authority (veterinary) that a turkey baster is an ideal way to administer liquid medication to your dog.

The last good-bye and the rainbow bridge

Bassets are known for their great courage and stoicism in the face of pain. It takes an equal courage on the part of the owner to know when it is time to say good-bye to our faithful pets. This, of course, is an individual decision, but I think we all know in our hearts when the moment has come. And that brings me to the story of the Rainbow Bridge.

In the Japanese Shinto religion, the Rainbow Bridge is the passageway to heaven. For animal lovers, it is a special place, too. The following story is a well-known tale, author unknown:

> *Just this side of heaven is a place called Rainbow Bridge. When an animal dies who has been especially close to someone on Earth, that pet goes to Rainbow Bridge. There are meadows and hills for all our special friends so they can run and play together. There is plenty of food, water, and sunshine, and our friends are warm and comfortable.*
>
> *All the animals who had been old and ill are restored to health and vigor; those who were hurt or maimed are made whole and strong again, just as we remember them in our dreams of times gone by. The animals are happy and content, except for one small thing; they each miss someone very special to them who had to be left behind. They all run and play together, but the day comes when one suddenly stops and looks into the distance. His bright eyes are intent; his eager body quivers. Suddenly he begins to run from the group, flying over the green grass, his legs carrying him faster and faster.*
>
> *You have been spotted, and when you and your special friend finally meet, you cling together in joyous reunion, never to be parted again. The happy kisses rain upon your face; your hands once again caress the beloved head, and you look once more into the trusting eyes of your pet, so long gone from your life, but never absent from your heart.*
>
> *Then you cross Rainbow Bridge together. . . .*

"Mom!"

The Basset Hound Owner

What's so great about owning a Basset Hound?

Everything! Here are some answers from the list:

> *Where else can you find that combination of speed, grace, beauty, intelligence, and unfailing obedience?—Sue Lockhart*

> *I have had various dogs and other pets over my lifetime, and Bassets seem to come closest to the ideals we would like in a friend. They give unconditional love and trust to their owners. In addition, they have humanlike qualities, both good and bad. They have more personality than any of God's other creatures. All from an animal who can only express himself with his tail.—David Derf*

> *I have to disagree here. For starters, Bassets express themselves with their eyes! You can tell whether they're happy, sad, or bored. Bassets DO smile, with their eyes. Look deep enough and you can tell.*
> *—Angelos Megremis*

Don't forget the ears. There's the normal position where they just sort of hang there, but when they are curious or interested in something, they cock them forward so that they flare out.—Jerry Evenden

I love their independence, faithfulness, inquisitiveness, stubbornness, clownishness, slowness, speed, friendliness, and love. Not a day goes by that they don't make me smile and make me scowl. There is not a single day that is dull in a house with Bassets. We fell head over heels in love with the clownish personality that can be so exasperating at times and so wonderful all the time. They are stubborn, slow, low, slobbering, and noisy. . . . I love every minute of them.—Lisa Slinsky

Basset ownership builds character. It makes you aware of your position on the food chain.—JoAnne Smith

Bassets are very lovable, sweet, smart, and so-o-o funny. I get more kisses from my Bassets than from my other dogs. They have good dispositions, they're happy all the time, and they get along with everybody and everything. I could go on and on.—Eva Wickemeier

Their ears are made for flopping; their bellies are made for rubbing; their noses are just right for kissing. They love cuddling and are very comforting in a sad time. They are natural clowns and psychologists; they know just how to manipulate you to get more food, a walk, your side of the bed—whatever. In short, they're perfect!—Amanda Sherwin

What would a wedding day be without a Basset in attendance? In fact, what would a cake be without a Basset to grace the top? (Donna Matushak and Robert Funk)

I prefer my Basset Hounds over any other breed (and I've had many) because of their quick wit. They are always the comedians who are ready to entertain. They are extremely loving, devoted, and great listeners. My Basset is always happy and is such a clown! She allows us to live with her! Let's not forget the sad droopy face that we cannot scold because it looks so pitiful. When I was in traction with a broken arm, Ashley the Basset didn't leave my side. She watched every move I made and every move someone else made around me. She guarded my broken arm better than I did. I couldn't imagine life without my Basset!—Karen Clemente

Neither, apparently, can Tracey Joscelyn:

My boyfriend finally came right out and said that he did not like my Basset, Darwin! He called him a slobbery, in-your-face, undisciplined hound! Well, I dumped him on the spot. Allegiance to the hound!!!

Karen Clemente has a devoted friend and guardian in Ashley.

Good for you, Tracey. All of us know there is something spooky about a person who can't love a Basset. After receiving many congratulations from the group on her loyalty to her dog, Tracey said, "The point is that I brought Darwin home when he was seven weeks old and told him that I would be his mum and take care of him until the day he died. I intend to keep that promise." Bravo.

I have never known another breed that has so many individuals and is so much fun to be around. I read today that laughter increases longevity by removing toxins. I guess my husband and I will live forever with the Bassets.—Susan Owen

Actually, I have found a medical use for Bassets. A while ago, when I did a little too much work in the garden, I was having some problems with a stiff back. It's truly amazing, but one of my friends put our Basset, Ruby, on my back, and she walked up and down for about five minutes. A Basset massage! Incredible, but my back problems were cured instantly!

Famous and infamous Basset Hound owners

Cokey Roberts (NPR and
  ABC news journalist)

Peter Falk (Actor)

General Lafayette

George Washington

Billy Carter

Troy Roberts (CBS news)

Tom T. Hall (C and W singer)

James Thurber (Humorist)

Rex Harrison (Actor)

Mary Tyler Moore (Actor)

Dukes of Hazard

Arthur Miller (Playwright)

Willard Scott (Weatherperson)

Bob Barker (Game show host)

Diedre Hall (Soap opera star)

Bob Hope

The Maytag Repair Man

Owners' Hall of Fame

One of my ideal owners is Melinda Brown, the woman who took in Chelsea, the blind Basset, as a foster dog and helped her achieve her Canine Good Citizen certificate.

Another of my heroes is Gretchen Laffert, who, when Miss Xanadu ruptured two disks in her back, would not accept the probability that her pet would never walk again. Gretchen took her to cold laser light therapy, chiropractic adjustment, and acupuncture. She writes:

> I started Xan on homeopathic remedies along with glandular supplements. I massaged her hind legs and back twice daily. We made her stand and attempt to walk with the aid of a sling made from an old sweatshirt. She went outside three or four times a day and struggled to keep her feet moving. It was a long and very cold winter, but I have never been so determined about anything as I was about Xanadu's recovery. Gradually, she was able to move her legs again. On May 12, 1996, my wonderful Miss Xanadu walked out the back door with the other dogs, stepped over the threshold of the back door, went down the deck of the back porch, and walked down the hill to the backyard. She performed her morning obligations, and then proceeded to walk up the hill, up the stairs to the deck, and back into the house. That day was better for me than Valentine's Day, Mother's Day, the Fourth of July, my birthday, and Christmas all rolled up into one. It was a very special day, a new beginning for my precious Miss Xanadu.

(This, by the way, was Miss Xanadu's second close brush; when she was a puppy, her brother was killed and she herself was made dangerously ill by a liberal dose of strychnine some psychopath threw into the puppies' pen.)

JoAnne Smith and Melissa Fenchel also make the grade. They adopted Katsie, a puppy mill victim:

> Five years ago we rescued her from a small-time puppy mill where she'd been bred every heat and was used up. When she had puppies, the owners would bring her into the house so they could show off for prospective buyers. When she didn't have puppies, she was kept in a

windowless shed surrounded by stockade fencing. She had over **one hundred puppies** *in her lifetime and was in such poor condition that the vet refused to give her inoculations. She had eye infections, gum infections, ear infections, and almost no hair. What hair there was was so coarse that she felt like a pig. Her teeth were covered with what looked like gray clay. Her back toenails were grown into her paw pads so that she walked on her rear hocks. Her front toenails were worn to the quick, but not from being clipped. Her puppies had been kept in a pen outside the shed, and she could hear them crying, so she tried to dig out and get to them. She had never worn a collar—her owner simply dragged her around by the skin on her neck. She slunk around, afraid of everyone and everything. Today Katsie, now happy and healthy, celebrated her eleventh birthday.*

Katsie recently passed away, and the 1997 Michigan Basset Waddle was held in her honor.

Belinda Lanphear had a similar experience with Nellie, a Christmas gift puppy who had outgrown her puppyhood. Before Belinda adopted her six years ago, Nellie was chained to her doghouse by a choke collar. Belinda says:

Nellie was a one-year-old nightmare, totally untrained, and had every imaginable bad habit. She most definitely was not housebroken, and she jumped, barked, chewed, pulled, pushed, and was a 45-pound pain-in-the-butt.

Belinda undertook a course of obedience training. Nellie has now earned her Companion Dog Excellent degree from the American Kennel Club (in 1995, only three Basset Hounds earned this degree). Even more impressive, Nellie has been featured in many television commercials and magazine advertisements. As Belinda says:

She loves the attention she gets on the set and the hot dogs she receives for jobs well done. And I love getting paid for doing something I love— working with my best friend.

Nellie's achievements are a great success story.

Unfortunately, Nellie has suffered an attack of acute glaucoma and has lost the sight in her right eye. Nellie's acting career is probably over, but Belinda is continuing her training and hopes to earn the Utility Dog certificate and a tracking title. Belinda owes Nellie a great deal:

She has been my sanity at insane times, my constant when chaos prevailed, my clown when my world needed laughter. I don't think I realized how much I loved her, and how much a part of my life she is, until I lost a small part of her.

The most recent additions to the Hall of Fame are our Canadian neighbors, Dawn and Mike O'Keeffe. They recently acquired Lucy, a paraplegic Basset from the state of Washington. Lucy, who is a six-year-old tricolor, had her back broken by an ill-tempered horse. Her owners made a two-wheeled cart to help her move around, but Lucy, although quite mobile, was unable to handle stairs and steep hills. She was scheduled to be euthanized, but her plight was publicized on Basset-L, and the O'Keeffes raced to the rescue. Lucy was flown into Detroit (airfare donated) after an unscheduled overnight stop in Utah. This was a difficult experience for Lucy as well as for the O'Keeffes and Michigan Basset Rescue, who helped arrange the logistics. The airline, which shall remain nameless, **lost** Lucy and could not understand why everyone was so upset over a piece of "cargo."

Lucy uses a two-wheeled cart to get around after her back was broken. Her owners, Dawn and Mike O'Keeffe, say they are determined to get her walking on her own again.

Lucy was finally recovered, however, and has now arrived in her new home in Canada. In the words of Dawn O'Keeffe:

> Lucy is home safe and sound, a little more traveled than we had hoped, but doing wonderfully. She has been eating well, seems quite comfortable with all of us, does her business outside, and has a great time chasing Bailey around the yard at full speed (when she doesn't hit a snowbank). Lucy does amazingly well in the cart, but we hate it. She moves her legs when we tickle her feet, so we are trying to find somewhere to take her for swimming therapy. We will do everything we can to get this little girl walking on her own again.

When we agree to get a dog, we are acquiring a child who will never grow up and go to college. He will never go out and get a job. Bassets are welfare cases. We indeed have a friend for life, but one who is utterly dependent upon us for his food, care, and well-being. Bassets are literally genetically altered creatures of our own making and cannot survive without our dedicated care. A Basset running around on his own would last about a week, even if he could find enough garbage to eat.

Bassets have all the emotions that we do—they love, they sulk, they get jealous, they feel afraid. And they suffer. The great British philosopher John Stuart Mill says that it is our mutual capacity for suffering that binds human beings and animals together. It also commands and requires us to treat our animal cousins kindly. The Buddha said the same. If we fail in our responsibility to our pet, we are guilty of committing a grave sin against a fellow sentient creature whom we have promised to love and care for. (I have it on good authority that the keepers of both the Pearly Gates and the Rainbow Bridge do not look kindly on this sort of behavior.)

The owners' self-test

No one reading this book, however, belongs to the category of bad owners. But what kind of owner are you? How do you regard your Basset? Give yourself this quiz to find out (please circle the best response):

1. My Basset:
   (a) is a lazy bum
   (b) likes to conserve his energy

2. My Basset:
   (a) is stubborn
   (b) knows his own mind

3. My Basset:
   (a) eats like a pig
   (b) is a connoisseur of good food

4. My Basset:
   (a) constantly gets underfoot
   (b) is always at my side

5. My Basset, described in a word, is:
   (a) annoying
   (b) divine

6. If my Basset is looking a little peaked, I:
   (a) pat him on the head and keep an eye on him
   (b) call the Surgeon General and demand service

7. When my Basset knocks over the trash and spreads it all over the kitchen floor, I:
   (a) scold him firmly
   (b) blame myself

8. During a conflict of interest over the couch, I:
   (a) generally come to an agreement with my Basset after a few moments of mutual butt-shoving
   (b) get a chair from the kitchen to sit on

9. When preparing my Basset's food, I:
   (a) make a healthy, nutritionally balanced meal
   (b) give him half my pizza

10. If I must go out and leave my Basset for a few hours, I:
    (a) make sure he has everything he needs, then go out and enjoy myself
    (b) call the neighbors every hour to go over and check on the dog

If you scored more "a"s than "b"s, you are a well-balanced, sane Basset owner. You should think about getting another one.

If you scored more "b"s than "a"s, you are deep in the grip of Basset-mania. The disease is apparently incurable, but not fatal. Enjoy your Basset, and get some more of them. You might as well.

GRACIE

Pam Posey-Tanzey

The Basset will reward you with love and joy and humor. These are life's greatest gifts.

We have read of the joys of the Basset,
We have examined each sparkling facet,
The ears, skin, and sound
Of this marvelous hound,
And it hasn't been too bad, now, has it?

Miles-Mugwump Personality Profile

Since we already know that the Basset is a medieval dog in looks, it is not surprising to learn that his temper and personality type are also, in many respects, medieval. I have discovered that the four basic Basset personality types (although each, of course, has infinite permutations) correspond with the medieval conception of humours—a theory of medicine gone sadly out of practice. The four humours are: blood (hot and moist—sanguine—snuggle Basset), phlegm (cold and moist—phlegmatic—iconoclastic Basset), yellow bile (hot and dry—choleric—demonic Basset), and black bile (cold and dry—melancholic—bizarre Basset). Ideally, the four humours should be in balance or harmony with each other; when one takes control, things start to go awry. All this sounds a bit mysterious, but if you replace the word "humour" with a more modern word—like "neurosis," for instance—all of a sudden it starts making a lot more sense.

Please circle the **most** applicable response to each question:

1. Given the choice, your Basset would rather:
   - (p) sleep
   - (m) run off
   - (s) cuddle up with you
   - (c) pee on the bed
   - (c) work on his stamp collection

2. When confronted with strange humans, your Basset:
   - (s) pretends they're long-lost relatives
   - (p) ignores them
   - (c) walks up to see if they have any food
   - (m) starts howling

3. Your Basset prefers to eat:
   - (s) underwear
   - (p) garbage
   - (c) choice steak
   - (m) disposable razors

4. In his relationship with other pets, your Basset:
   - (p) ignores them
   - (m) barks at them
   - (s) cuddles up to them
   - (c) tries to get them sent off to the SPCA

"Explain in 50 words or less, why you should be teacher's pet."

5. When you're not home, your Basset will most likely:

(m) sleep the entire time, so as to be ready to tear the house apart on your return

(c) tear the house apart, so as to be ready to sleep the entire time after you're home

(p) do nothing

(s) watch television

6. When confronted with a much larger, meaner dog, your Basset:

(m) runs away

(m) crawls around on the ground like a slave

(c) stands behind you, using you as a shield, and growls ferociously

(p) pretends he doesn't see the other dog

(s) tries to make friends with the other dog

7. In relationships with the opposite sex, your Basset:

(s) is a regular Romeo/Juliet

(m) seems terrified

(p) ignores the other dog

(c) attacks without warning

8. Among the family members, your Basset:

(m) definitely prefers one person

(s) loves everyone equally wildly

(p) is affectionate, but is not brimming with passion

(c) prefers to be alone

9. Your Basset is most terrified of:

(c) getting his nails clipped

(s) going to the vet

(p) getting a bath

(s) being left alone for five minutes

(m) thunder

(s) vacuum cleaners

10. When you call your Basset to come, he:

(s) trots up immediately, tail wagging

(m) comes reluctantly, after being repeatedly yelled at

(p) doesn't move

(c) runs off in the opposite direction

11. When you scold your Basset, he
    (m) pees on the floor
    (s) looks sad and guilty
    (s) tries to kiss you
    (p) stares at you blankly
    (c) gives you a dirty look and stalks off

12. Where does your Basset Hound sleep?
    (p) in his own bed
    (s) in your bed
    (s, p, m, c) on the couch
    (m) on your lap
    (c) wherever is most incon-venient for you

13. Does your Basset consider you to be:
    (s) his mother
    (s) his best friend
    (c) his servant
    (p) not worth talking to
    (m) someone who might do something strange to him at any moment

14. When you are ill, your Basset is most likely to:
    (s) hover by your side in sympathetic concern

    (m) race around the house barking loudly
    (p) ignore you
    (m) want to be taken out
    (c) hope it's not catching and start looking for another home

15. If teased by children, your Basset most likely will:
    (s) play good-naturedly with them
    (p) ignore them and hope they'll go home soon
    (m) snarl and snap in the air
    (c) kill the brats

16. Which of the following adjec-tives **best** describes your Bas-set Hound?
    (m) stubborn
    (p) lazy
    (s) friendly
    (c) satanic

17. When your Basset gets away, he usually goes:
    (s) next door
    (m) across the street
    (c) as far as he can get
    (p) nowhere

Results

Which letter turned up most frequently in your responses? (The more frequent the letter, the stronger the correlation between your Basset and his medieval type.)

If you . . .

Scored mostly "s": You own a snuggle Basset, corresponding to the medieval "sanguine" or "blood" type. This is the kind of dog who can make you money in television commercials. He is a warm, generous being who idolizes you. Your main problem is how to keep this creature from smothering you in bed at night with his kisses.

Scored mostly "m": You are living in an uneasy truce with the dreaded mad Basset, or bizarre Basset, corresponding to the medieval "melancholic" type, overstocked with black bile. All Bassets have a trace of bizarre-ity, but your Hound is experiencing an overload.

Scored mostly "p": You are owned by an iconoclastic Basset, a strong, individualistic, self-sufficient hound, corresponding to the medieval "phlegmatic" type. As his name signifies, this Basset also tends to drool a lot, due to the excess phlegm produced.

Scored mostly "c": Your Basset is possessed by a demon. Perform appropriate rites. The demon manifests itself with a superfluity of yellow bile, resulting in the "choleric" Basset.

ELEVEN

Basset Resources

Basset Clubs

American Kennel Club (AKC)
212-692-8200

Call for the most recent information about whom to contact about the local club in your area.

Basset Hound Club of America
Melody Fair, Secretary
P.O. Box 339
Noti, OR 97461
E-mail: Heirline@aol.com

Check the following list for the name of a Basset Hound Club near you.

Arizona:
Valley Del Sol BHC

California:
BHC of Greater San Diego

BHC of Sacramento
BHC of Southern California
BHC Northern California

Colorado:
Timberline BHC

Florida:
South Florida BHC
Suncoast BHC

Hawaii:
BHC of Hawaii

Illinois:
Fort Dearborn BHC
Lincoln Land BHC

Indiana:
BHC of Central Indiana

Kentucky:

Kentuckiana BHC

Maryland:

BHC of Maryland, Inc.

Massachusetts:

Pilgrim BHC

Michigan:

BHC of Greater Detroit
Looking Glass BHC
Western Michigan BHC

Minnesota:

Greater Minneapolis-St. Paul
BHC

New Jersey:

Partroon BHC

New York:

Capital District BHC

Ohio:

Maumee Valley BHC

Oklahoma:

BHC of Tulsa

Oregon:

BHC of Portland, Oregon,
Inc.
Emerald Empire BHC

Pennsylvania:

Berkshire Valley BHC

Buckeye BHC
Lenape BHC
Rancocas Valley BHC
Susquehanna BHC
Valley Forge BHC

Texas:

BHC of Greater Fort Worth
BHC of Greater Houston
BHC of San Antonio
Dal-Tex BHC (Dallas)
Highland Lakes BHC

**Virginia, Maryland,
Washington, DC:**

Potomac Basset Hound Club

Washington:

BHC of Greater Seattle

Wisconsin:

Badgerland BHC

Canada:

Canadian Kennel Club
80 Skyway Avenue
Etobicoke, Ontario
Canada M9W 6R4

BHC of British Columbia

BHC of Canada
Pat Nurse
588 Pinewood St.
Oshawa, ON LIG 254
905-723-7668

Magazines and Journals

Special issues:

Life magazine (May 1997): Features the Michigan Basset Waddle.

Dog Fancy (June 1997): Features the Basset Hound.

Bugler (published since 1968): Appears monthly. $20.00 per year subscription. Contains health tips, show news, black-and-white photos. Riche Churchill, Editor. 5972 Francis Ferry Rd., McMinnville, TN 37110. 615-686-2012.

Tally-Ho: The official publication of the Basset Hound Club of America. Monthly. Free with membership. For nonmembers, $35.00 per year. Show news, health tips, etc. Black-and-white photos. Carolyn Young, Editor. P.O. Box 841, Ridgefield, WA 98642. Phone: 360-887-4520. Fax: 360-887-3669. E-mail:rayoung@ix.netcom.com.

AKC Gazette. American Kennel Club. 51 Madison Ave., New York, NY 10010.

Books

Braun, Mercedes. *The New Complete Basset Hound*, 4th edition. New York: Howell Book House, 1979.

Camino, E.E. *Basset Hound Champions, 1952–1992*. Camino Book Company, 1996.

Foy, Marcia A and Nicholas, Anna Katherine. *The Basset Hound*. Neptune, N.J.: Tfh Publications, 1985.

Stahlkuppe, Joe. *Basset Hounds: Everything About Purchase, Nutrition, Breeding, Behavior, and Training*. Hauppauge, N.Y.: Barron's Educational Series, 1997.

Walton, Margaret S. *The New Basset Hound*. New York: Howell Book House, 1993.

Wicklund, Barbara. *The Basset Hound: An Owner's Guide to a Happy Healthy Pet*. New York: Howell Book House, 1996.

Video

AKC Video: Breed Standard Series—*The Basset Hound*

> AKC/Video Fulfillment
> 5580 Centerview Dr.
> Suite 200
> Raleigh, NC 27606

Supplies and Catalogs

Omaha Vaccines
800-367-4444

In the Company of Dogs: Dog items.
P.O. Box 7071
Dover, DE 19903
800-924-5050

R.C. Steele: Wholesale Pet and Animal Care Supplies
800-872-3773

Pedigrees: Pet Catalog
1989 Transit Way
P.O. Box 905
Brockport, NY 14420-0905
800-548-4786

J.B. Wholesale Pet Supplies, Inc.
5 Raritan Rd.
Oakland, NJ 07436
800-526-0388

Discount Master: Animal Care Catalog
Humbolt Industrial Park
1 Maple Wood Dr.
Hazleton, PA 18201-9798
800-346-0749

Valley Vet Supply
East Hwy. 36
P.O. Box 504
Marysville, KS 66508-0504
800-360-4838

Direct Book Service
Dog & Cat Book Catalog
P.O. Box 2778
Wenatchee, WA 98807-2778
800-776-2665
E-mail: dgctbook@cascade.net

Pet-Pak, Inc.
(First aid kits for pets)
P.O. Box 982
Edison, NJ 08818-0982
908-906-9200
800-217-PETS (7387)

Internet Web Sites

American Kennel Club Basset Hound Breed Standard: http://www.akc.org/basset.htm

Basset Hound Club of America Home Page: http://www.princeton.edu~nadelman/bhca/bhca/html

The Basset Hound FAQ: http://www.zmall.com/pet_talk/dog-faqs/breeds/bassets.html

Compiled by Judy Trenck with help from Mary Louise Chipman and Judi Kinnear. Not only contains lots of interesting facts about Basset personalities and tips for their care, but provides valuable links to many other sites on the Web.
Basset-L Official Web site (includes a free newsgroup): http://www/execpc.com/dderf/basset-l

Bassetopia: http://www.ccmi1.com/basset/

The Basset's Den: http://www/mainelink.net/~writer/basset/Basset_home.html

Contains stories, a recorded HOWL, adoption information, and a gallery of photos from around the world.

The Daily Drool Home Page: http://users.aol.combassethome

Contains a Basset photo album and information on how to subscribe free to *The Daily Drool,* a Basset newsletter. The *Daily Drool* (Nancy Gallagher, administrator) is an Internet mail group devoted entirely to those lovable Basset Hounds and their families.

Debbie's Basset Hound Page: http://www/geocities.com/Heartland/4788/basset.html

Contains Basset Hound chat. Provides hyperlinks to Basset Hound information.

BROOD—Basset Rescue of Old Dominion:
http://www.web ventures.com/basset/brood.html. 703-455-9656.

Rescue Organizations

AKC Companion Animal Recovery: Offers 24-hour, 365-day-a-year service to help to find and identify your lost pet. It costs nine dollars a year to register with the service. 800-252-7894. This service coordinates several individual registries.

State by State

California:

Basset Hound Rescue of
Southern California
Adrianne Sherard
562-690-4579
E-mail: sherard@cogent.net

Northern California
Ruth Wilcox
510-562-1906

San Diego Basset Hound
Rescue
Jerri Caswell
P.O. Box 601304
San Diego, CA 92160
619-286-8638

Colorado:

High Country Basset Hound
Rescue and Adoption Service
Theo Clark, President
4418 Rosecrown Ct.
Fort Collins, CO 80526
970-530-7332

Joanne Keiderling (dog
placements)
303-795-6153

Mary Mosley (lost and found)
303-421-4258
E-mail
mosleyjm@worldnet.att.net

Connecticut:

Marilyn Conklyn
860-434-2767

Florida:

Nancy Bressler (Melbourne)
407-259-3400

Kay Robertson (Ft. Lauderdale)
954-772-3014

Tish Lee (Jacksonville)
904-264-4020

Geneva and David Kosh
(Tampa)
813-920-6119

Cindy and Scott Moyer
(Tampa)
813-677-5136

Brenda Oliver (Daytona Beach)
904-424-1699

Georgia:

Basset Hound Rescue of Georgia
Julie Bradley
5006 Melanie Dr.
Kennesaw, GA 30144
Phone: 770-499-1164
Fax: 770-955-1156
E-mail: jkbradl@aol.com

Illinois:

Guardian Angel Basset Rescue
Fran Gray
185 E. 34th St.
S. Chicago Heights, IL 69411
708-758-7455

Indiana:

Indiana Basset Rescue
Sally Allen
P.O. Box 1256
Carmel, IN 46032

Iowa:

Linda Rudolph
515-834-2382

Kansas:

Kim Dunn
913-557-5224

Michigan:

Western Michigan Basset Rescue
Gretchen Laffert
616-281-2338
E-mail: glaffert@concentric.net

Michigan Basset Rescue
Melissa Fenchel
810-623-1698
E-mail: bassetrescue@mindsprin

Montana:

Montana Basset Rescue
Donna Owens
1695 River Road West
Plains, MT 59859
406-826-4544

Mark and Amy Beth Henson
P.O. Box 553
East Helena, MT 59635
E-mail: Houndage@aol.com

Nebraska:

Eastern Nebraska Basset
Rescue
402-263-5046

New England:

Pilgrim Basset Rescue
Linda Fowler
Fall River, MA
508-672-6780

**New York, New Jersey,
Pennsylvania:**

Tri-State Basset Rescue
League, Inc.
Barbara Wicklund
1737 Route 206
Skillman, NJ 08558
908-464-0956

North and South Carolina:

Carolina Rescue League
Lisa Lamoreux
8655 Harvell Rd.
Concord, NC 28025
704-455-2643

Francena Morrissey
17 Renwick Ct.
Raleigh, NC 27615
919-676-0616

Ohio:

Eva Wick
987 Lila Ave.
Milford, OH 45150
513-248-1177

Oregon:

Emerald Empire Basset Hound
Rescue
Renee Bender
541-863-4557

Tennessee:

Tennessee Valley Basset
Rescue
Martha Huffman
2880 Highway 81 N
Fall Branch, TN 37656
423-348-7512

Texas:

North Texas Basset Rescue
Sharon Nance
17 Creekmere Dr.
Trophy Club, TX 76262
517-430-0407

Basset Hound Club of Greater
Fort Worth, Rescue Committee
Harriet Richman
1416 W. Jeter Rd.
Argyle, TX 76266
817-240-3212

Virginia, West Virginia, Maryland:

Basset Rescue of Old Domin-
ion (BROOD)
Melinda Brown
9617 Villagesmith Way
Burke, VA 22015
703-455-9656
E-mail:
SARABRWN@aol.com

Washington:

Alexa Paul

425-481-7309

Wisconsin:

Badgerland Basset Hound
Club, Rescue Committee
Jane Baetz
2135 Granville Rd.
West Bend, WI 53095
414-375-2522

Activities Organizations

U.S. Dog Agility Association, Inc.
P.O. Box 850955
Richardson, TX 75085-0955
214-231-9700

The American Kennel Club
ATTN: Canine Good Citizen
Certificate
5580 Centerview Dr., Suite 2200
Raleigh, NC 27606-3390
919-233-9780

Other Organizations

Orthopedic Foundation for
Animals (OFA)
(Hip registry)
2300 E. Nifong Blvd.
Columbia, MO 65201-3856

American Dog Trainer's Network
161 West 4th St.
New York, NY 10014
212-727-7257

Association of Pet Dog Trainers
P.O. Box 3734
Salinas, CA 93912
408-663-9257

National Association of Dog
Obedience Instructors
2286 East Steel Rd.
St. Johns, MI 48879

Therapy Dogs International
6 Hilltop Rd.
Mendham, NJ 07945

5 383